D1193854

JEWS IN THE ARTS AND SCIENCES

JUBILEE VOLUME

JEWISH ACADEMY OF ARTS AND SCIENCES

EDITORIAL COMMITTEE

MORDECAI SOLTES, *Chairman*

HYMEN ALPERN

ABRAHAM BURSTEIN

LEO JUNG

HERALD SQUARE PRESS, INC.
233 Spring Street, New York 13, N.Y.

Contents

Preface

THE ISSUANCE of this Jubilee Volume marks the completion of a quarter of a century of valuable and diversified services rendered by the Jewish Academy of Arts and Sciences. Organized in 1927 as an honor society of American Jews who had attained distinction in the arts, sciences and professions, it has enjoyed the leadership of the following scholars who have served as presidents of this Academy: Drs. Henry Keller, Morris Raphael Cohen, Chaim Tchernowitz and Leo Jung. In addition to its regular membership and fellows there are corresponding members throughout the world.

The following objectives of the Academy were set forth when it was founded:

1. To encourage, support, and promote among Jews throughout the world, the advancement of the arts, sciences, and all other departments of knowledge.
2. To encourage, stimulate, and promote the interchange of views on all branches of learning, with particular reference to those bearing on Jewish life and thought.
3. To cultivate, promote, and maintain friendly and social intercourse among its members.
4. To use, as means to the aforesaid ends, research, publication, discussion, the establishment and maintenance of friendly relations with other academies, societies, and institutions of learning throughout the world, and any other means and agencies which from time to time shall be expedient.

Public meetings are held four times annually, at which new members are inducted and written discourses read and discussed. Most of the latter which are included in this volume have been synopsized. At the end will be found lists of the present officers, board of governors, members and fellows, and the titles of the addresses presented at the meetings held since 1934.

MORDECAI SOLTES

JEWISH WRITERS IN LATIN AMERICAN LITERATURE

BY DR. HYMEN ALPERN

Jewish Writers in
Latin American Literature

BY DR. HYMEN ALPERN

WHILE BOATLOADS of victims of Ferdinand and Isabella's decree of expulsion were sailing eastward from Spanish ports in 1492, three other boats sailed westward to an unknown destination. Jewish scientists had a leading role in making this possible; the money for the expedition was Jewish, although credit was given to the queen; the great Admiral was probably of Jewish descent, and several of his adjutants were also Jews, masquerading as Christians. Those bound eastward thus had their avantcouriers heading westward.

By 1625 there were already at Recife, Brazil, nearly 5000 Jews. These early settlers were in the main Sephardic refugees from the Inquisition. Before long, however, they were either destroyed by it or absorbed into the Indo-Hispanic Christian communities as *conversos.*

These early Jewish settlers in the Spanish and Portuguese New World colonies continued their tradition of literary collaboration in the languages of the Iberian Peninsula. Two outstanding figures during the colonial period were Luis de Carvajal and Antonio José da Silva, the first in Spanish and the second in Portuguese.

Luis de Carvajal was a nephew of the governor of the Mexican province of Nuevo León and the most distinguished of the *marranos* in New Spain, as colonial Mexico was known. The younger Carvajal was executed at an *auto da fé* in Mexico City in 1596. His confession, written by him while in an Inquisition dungeon, accredits him as the first Jewish author in the New World. His travails and those of his fellow *marranos* are echoed in the hymns and dirges he composed for the Jewish festivals and fasts.

3

In 1939 all of Brazil observed the bicentenary of the death at the Inquisition stake in Lisbon of the father of its national theatre, Antonio José da Silva o Judeu (the Jew). This gifted writer, born in Brazil in 1705, burned by the Inquisition "for writing satirical poems and for observing the Mosaic laws," was a prolific and versatile poet. He was styled "the Portuguese Plautus" and his comedies were popularly referred to as *As óperas do Judeu*—the Jew's operas.

An early master in Hispanic-American letters after independence from the motherland was the continent's greatest 19th century novelist, Jorge Isaacs, the son of a British-Jewish father and a Colombian mother. His artistic novel *María* (1867) is a Latin-American classic. It has been more widely read and studied than any other written in Spanish America and has been translated into several languages. This masterpiece of the sentimental romantic school presents a powerful picture of home life on a Colombian plantation. Latin-American critics have noted the Hebraic as well as Colombian inspiration in its portrayal of patriarchal family life. Don Luis Alberto Sánchez, the noted literary critic and historian, remarks about "a note of intimate tenderness which gives *María* the certain fascination of the ever-lasting, of that which does not die, of that which will not die. And the feeling for the landscape, which he endows with a human quality, is also Hebraic."

The reappearance of Jews in mass in the Hispanic world started in the late 1890's in Argentina with Baron de Hirsch's colonization project. This second encounter between the Hispanic and Jewish worlds introduced the Ashkenazic Jews to the Spanish-speaking scene. In present day Argentina the Sephardim are only about a fifth of the Jewish community, which numbers around half a million. Jewish communities of varying sizes dot the map of Latin America from the Río Grande and the Caribbean Islands to the Straits of Magellan.

It is noteworthy that the Jewish contribution to Latin-American letters does not come from the Sephardic Jews, who have preserved for centuries the Spanish language and the Judeo-Spanish cultural tradition, but from Ashkenazim. The adaptation and assimilation of these immigrants from East Europe and of their Argentine-born children raised in a Yiddish speaking immigrant environment into the cultural as well as the economic life of their new land has been amazing. It is particularly gratifying that this "assimilation" of the Argentine group of Jewish-Spanish writers did not, for the most part, involve a rejection of their Jewish heritage.

The Spanish works of these Jewish writers, either born abroad themselves or the first generation born on Argentine soil, really constitute a hymn of gratitude to the freedom and human dignity they and their people found on the Argentine pampas after liberation from the lands of oppression. Their writings not only reveal the transformation within the Jewish group; they transcend the limits of the immigrant enclave, reflecting universal horizons, and very significantly are from the start an enrichment of Argentine letters. This much can be gathered from the fact that in an anthology of Argentine short stories, published in Buenos Aires, out of 28 authors represented, eight are Jews. For three successive years Jewish writers won the first municipal prize for poetry in the capital city, as well as one in the drama and a third prize in fiction. Their preeminence is not only numerical. Qualitatively they rank high. Thus one of the best prose stylists in Argentine literature is universally recognized to be Alberto Gerchunoff; a most successful playwright is Samuel Eichelbaum; one of the most distinguished poets is Israel Zeitlin, known by his nom de plume, César Tiempo. Among the masters of the spoken Castilian word are the eloquent political orator, Enrique Dickmann, the celebrated actress, Paulina Singermann, and her sister Berta, famous throughout the Spanish-speaking world, including Spain, as the virtuoso diseuse and recitalist of verse.

The remarkably successful and rapid acclimatization of the Askenazim to the language and culture of the Hispanic world is exemplified by none better than by the pioneer and until his recent death the dean of Argentine-Jewish writers in Spanish, Alberto Gerchunoff. He was the first among the immigrant generation to express in the language of the adopted land the experience of transplantation and the deep sentiment of the new attachment. This he did in his *Los Gauchos Judíos* (1910), a volume of stories and sketches of life in the Jewish agricultural settlements on the pampa, in which he himself had grown up to the age of seventeen. But Gerchunoff soon became an important figure in the general literature of Argentina. For many years until his death he was the chief editorial writer of one of the country's most influential dailies, *La Nación*. Throughout the Spanish speaking world—in Europe as well as in America—his mastery of Castilian prose was acclaimed in the short story as well as the essay. He was a member of the Argentine Academy of Letters, held professorships of literature, won national literary prizes, and served as president of an inter-American writers' congress.

Gerchunoff's life-long preoccupation with the problems of Hispanic tradition and culture and with those of Argentine society—areas in which he attained to eminent spokesmanship—did not estrange him entirely from Jewish interests. He never masked his origin by Hispanizing his name as other Jewish writers of his country have done. However, it required the holocaust and the soul stirring emergence of Israel to re-enlist him in full measure in Jewish ranks. His powerful word served in the cause against Nazism, and his winged Castilian prose carried understanding of the Jewish renaissance in Israel. In the latter field he collaborated loyally and effectively with the Jewish Agency.

Enrique Espinosa was born Shmuel Glusberg in Kishinev, Ukraine, in 1898. He has done a great deal for the dissemination of good literature, Jewish and non-Jewish, in all of Latin America and especially in Chile, where his publishing house, *Casa Editorial Babel,* has been active for years. Glusberg-Espinosa entered upon the literary scene in Spanish while still a resident of Argentina, where he was the founder and first secretary of the "Argentine Society of Writers." Among his better known works of a general nature are *Vida de San Martín* (Life of San Martin), Argentina's national hero; his *Cuentos Judíos* (Jewish Tales); and translations from the works of W. H. Hudson and Waldo Frank.

Max Dickmann was born in Buenos Aires in 1902, of immigrant parents. Yet his novel, *Madre América* (Mother America), the second of a trilogy, was awarded the Municipal Prize in literature on the basis of exemplary prose and interpretative power revealed in the treatment of the theme. The series is a portrayal of contemporary middle-class society of Buenos Aires. Its author, though a son of immigrants, derived from a cultural and linguistic medium so alien to the Latin clime of the great Plate River metropolis, was successful in becoming the spokesman of "Mother America."

In the drama, as well as in novel and essay, Jewish writers in Spanish have won a place of eminence for themselves in Argentina. It is the consensus of those best qualified to judge, that first place among contemporary Spanish-American dramatists belongs to Samuel Eichelbaum, a son of East European immigrants, born in 1894 in Domínguez, Entre Ríos, in the heart of the Jewish agricultural settlements.

Eichelbaum has been hailed by authoritative critics both for technical competence and profundity of dramatic thought, for changing the theatre of manners into one of problems, and for deepening its probing into the subconscious. He has written more than thirty plays and has won triumphs not only as the author of dramatic literature but also as the creator of effective, convincing and appealing stage works. Among his successes have been *La Tormenta de Dios* (God's Torment) and *Señorita,* both of which won first prizes in municipal literary awards. Eichelbaum has also written critical essays and short stories. Some of the latter have a Jewish background and theme. The locale of one of the best of them, *Una Buena Cosecha* (A Good Harvest) is in the Jewish agricultural colony of Rosh Piná.

César Tiempo, the famous literary name by which Israel Zeitlin is known, is another Jewish dramatist who has been acclaimed on the Argentine stage. His outstanding successes have been *El Teatro Soy Yo* (I Am the Theatre) and *Pan Criollo* (American Bread), both ranking high in dramatic quality and poetic values, treating Jewish themes with nobility and sincerity.

But Tiempo is above all a poet. Born in the Ukraine in 1906, he came to America as a young boy when his family joined in the migration to the pampa. The sensitivity to the lot of the Jew in an alien world which he brought with him from the pogrom-scarred Ukrainian Pale, he has integrally conserved in the New World. Thus he is one of the most Jewishly conscious writers in Castilian in Argentina. Zeitlin-Tiempo is also one of the wonders of the magic acclimatization in the Hispanic medium. He was only seventeen years old when he stirred the wonder of Buenos Aires critics with his first volume of poetry, entitled *Versos de Una por Clara Baker*. It was the suppleness with which the young foreign-born poet manipulated the rich Castilian language to give expression to new nuances of feeling that en-thused critic and reader alike.

That Tiempo has been able to win municipal literary awards of Buenos Aires for poetry volumes thematically Jewish would indicate that he was a genuine and gifted poet in his acquired language, so rich in great masters of poetic expression. In 1930 he won a prize for his *Libro para la Pausa del Sábado* (A Book for the Sabbath Pause). This volume was followed in 1933 by another, *El Sabatión Argentino* (Argentine Sabbatyon). César Tiempo has not only introduced a new theme into Argentine poetry. He has succeeded in the inner amalgam of language and sensitivity and thought. Brooding, sadness, undertones of melancholy, mystic feeling—these are innate characteristics of the Spanish language and the poetry expressed in it. Tiempo master-fully makes Spanish poesy the vehicle of his Jewish emotional burden.

César Tiempo has never been exclusively concerned with his own literary creativity. As editor and publisher of the magazine "*Columna,*" Tiempo has been a literary catalytic agent, ever ready to release and encourage creative talents wherever he discovered or suspected their existence. As a journalist contribu-ting to the two great Buenos Aires dailies, *La Prensa* and *La Nación*, he has been a stout-hearted champion of human rights and dignity, and in the forefront of the battle against intoler-ance, whether it be anti-Semitism or aimed at other minority targets.

A name that promises to eclipse many of the earlier Jewish Argentine poets is Carlos M. Grunberg, a native son of Buenos Aires. His exquisite satirical verses entitled *Mester de Judería* express his soul-seared indignation against Hitlerism. He has done beautiful translations of Heinrich Heine. A few years ago he founded a literary review, *Heredad.*

The foregoing writers are but a few selected from a larger number as representative of the cultural collaboration of the Jewish community with its adopted land. But it would be wrong to consider their work as for "export" only to their non-Jewish environment as a token of appreciation for a haven. These writers are fulfilling the need for self-expression of South American Jewry, which is increasingly becoming Spanish-speaking and thinking.

Thus from the very beginnings of Latin-American literature, the Jews have contributed out of all proportion to their numbers and in a most active and fructifying manner. In Latin America, as everywhere, the Jews carry hither and thither the pollen of thought.

This contribution is not merely the contribution of men of genius who are Jews by accident of birth; it is a Jewish contribution—of the Jewish heritage and of Jewish ideals. From Carvajal, writing under the shadow of the Inquisition, to César Tiempo, writing under the shadow of Perón, the Jewish Latin-American writers have contributed to Latin-American literature a sincerity and nobility of purpose, and a moral intensity characteristic of the Hebrew prophets. And this Hebraic tendency to look at the world through moral spectacles has not diminished their ability to depict the Latin-American scene but has rather enhanced their power to interpret and voice Latin-American strivings and hopes. And finally Jewish Latin-American writers have not been reluctant to deal with specific Jewish problems as affected by the Latin-American environment.

JUDAIC ELEMENTS IN EARLY AMERICAN LITERATURE

BY RABBI ABRAHAM BURSTEIN

Judaic Elements in
Early American Literature

BY RABBI ABRAHAM BURSTEIN

THAT WHICH we choose to call the Puritan tradition in American literature is actually Jewish. In literature and in life the Old Testament heritage remained astoundingly potent until approximately the middle of the nineteenth century. The process was facilitated by the King James version of the Bible, of which it has been said that its cadences, its music, its phraseology sank into the mind of the English-speaking reader and became part of his being.

The Puritan tradition laid the same stress on general free education for all that has always marked the life of the Jew in every land. When in 1670 Governor Berkeley of Virginia expressed his happiness that there were no free schools in his colony, he went counter to the entire tenor of colonial thought.

That the literary style of early American writing is biblical, and therefore Hebraic, is attested by the roll and balance of the sentences by George Washington and others of our early great men, in emulation of the King James version.

That the Bible was the prime inspiration of the literature of the period, is evidenced by the choice of a version of the Psalms as the first book to be published in the colonies. The "Bay Psalm Book" (1640) is otherwise a poor versification of the original. Not until 1662 did another volume come from an American press—this was "The Day of Doom," which with its stern warning to sinners expressed the Christian interpretation of the Old Testament. Most Christians ignored the exhortations to Israel to find joy in life and the festivals, but preferred to consider

13

the divine and prophetic objurgations against the sinning as Israel's basic biblical teaching.

But it is in a related field that Jewish influence was most strongly felt. The Talmud, under biblical prompting and exegesis, had combined the offices of clergy and magistracy (Sanhedrin), and so did the American colonials. The clergyman was the judge, and never a venal politician. Just as Jewish parents have long exerted every effort to provide their children with a Hebrew education, so that they might be able to read the prayerbook and Scripture, the Puritans also insisted on general education to assure competent reading of the sacred books. In these and many other matters early American life proved similar to traditional Jewish life in all times. And the effect of the relationship was strongly marked among Christian speakers and writers of the period.

Many of these merit lengthy mention, but their Judaic influences are all that require reference in this discussion. Thus, Cotton Mather (1663-1728) prayed every day, fasted twice a week or thereabout, and believed in witchcraft, like many a pious Jew of the past; yet, just like the observant Jewish doctors some of us may know, accepted the findings of science and supported such medical discoveries as vaccination.

There was Jonathan Edwards, great preacher, who, with all his piety, was not averse to composing an epithalamium to a bride which described all her physical charms. In this he was but employing the form of the Song of Songs, considered a sacred work despite intimate physical references to the heroine thereof. The Old Testament was his literary exemplar. One may mention also John Woolman (1720-1772), the Quaker diarist, whose words against exploitation of the poor, war, and the misuse of wealth, sound like the fulminations of the Prophets. Benjamin Franklin is reported to have had access to a volume of talmudic aphorisms in translation; the everyday virtues described in Poor Richard's Almanac are indeed in the genre of the Talmud and of Proverbs.

The end of the eighteenth century found the essentially Jewish religious motif dropping away from American literature, but in early nineteenth century transcendentalism and its neo-Platonism one can discover many Jewish elements, including also the Kabbalah. A Unitarian minister such as Ralph Waldo Emerson (1803-1882) could impress readers as a veritable Old Testament rhapsodist and psalmist, with his declaration that "every soul is of divine essence" and his presentation of the Oversoul as a connecting link among men.

It can be shown that Thoreau's emphasis on the simple virtues are a reflection of Jewish literary attitudes. Hawthorne displayed a Judaic obsession with the problem of evil: "The Scarlet Letter" brought up the physical punishment for guilt; "The House of the Seven Gables," ancestral guilt; and "The Marble Faun," the stirring of conscience. Melville's works, including "Moby Dick," were often examples of biblical poetry. Longfellow's moralizing can be traced to Judaic forbears. Even Lowell's bookishness and humanitarianism indicate a similar origin. And Whittier's hymns against slavery might have been thundered forth by one of the prophets.

The new motifs that came with Whitman and Mark Twain ended the more or less direct influence of the Judaic heritage on American men of letters.

Strangely enough, there were no Jewish writers before, let us say, 1925, who were imbued with the same tendencies that Judaized so much of early American literature. Only in these days are men like Ludwig Lewisohn groping their way back to those influences which first shaped the literature of the land in which Jewish authors are now living and prospering.

NOTES ON A TOUR OF ISRAEL

BY RABBI ABRAHAM BURSTEIN

Notes on a Tour of Israel

BY RABBI ABRAHAM BURSTEIN

THERE ARE two besetting sins of reports published by travelers to the new State of Israel. Many heed the exhortations of the late Chief Rabbi Kook and other religious leaders, and offer nothing but an uncritical, multi-adjectived eulogy of everything concerned with the land. Others wax unduly thoughtful, and seek to uncover the profound philosophical, psychological, cultural, and social forces animating the nation's existence. Yet random and even apparently superficial comments of the honest observer may bring one closer to the truth than attempts at fine and recondite writing.

Despite evidence of religious non-observance among many groups, and even active opposition to religion by extremists, there is enough observance in the land to designate it as essentially a religious country. One gains the impression, in the face of other interpretations, that if the largely irreligious Mapai chose the Religious Bloc to form a coalition government, this was not due entirely to political or other expediency, but to a lurking affection for the modes of the fathers found in the heart of most of the "religion-is-the-opium-of-the-people" Jewish Marxists.

I saw the land less than a year after the 1948 war with the Arabs. Yet the people, thinking only in terms of peace, expected travelers to say that their outstanding impression of the land was the physical development of the country and its colonies, the achievements of the newly formed government, the brightness and aptitude of the great crop of youngsters, or other peacetime evidences. So far has the ingrained Jewish love of peace entered into the spirits of a nation still embattled.

19

This feeling is all the more remarkable if one remembers that in 1949 one could look everywhere upon thousands of bulletholes, unrepaired or completely demolished structures, deserted Arab villages, protective walls and sandbags before every edifice, and roads lined with the skeletons of armored cars. Everyone was still talking of the treachery of the British, who would disarm a truck-load of Jewish boys and girls along the road, and then beckon to the lurking Arabs to cut the throats of the defenseless young people. They still recalled the promises of the Arab high command to their people who were urged to leave the warring country, that on their return they would have the choice of all Jewish women and property.

Almost every father or mother had the picture of a son or daughter to show—either dead or remarkable for some heroic feat. But there were no tears, even when an only child had been cut down—all eyes looked to the future. Such hopefulness in the past has in fact kept Jewry alive in every period of destruction and pogromization.

In Nazareth and elsewhere the existence of large Arab groups and labor unions side by side with the Jews gave the lie to the enemies who were shouting that Jewry was bent on annihilating all Arab peoples.

The reputed Jewish propensity for speechmaking is evident not alone in the Knesset, but in every colony one may visit. There are always representatives to address the visitors, to ask for American financial help and the sons and daughters of America.

Travel was extensive and difficult. Roads and communications were broken. Taxes were high, wages low. Subsistence without packages from America was difficult. Yet the general contentment was far higher than those who listened to the inevitable griping might suppose. Young children were convinced that no one on earth lived as well as they. "Why should I want to go to America?" was their reply to queries. "What have they in America that I can't find right here in my kevutzah?" Juvenile discipline was as a whole excellent, promising much for the future of the State.

There was no fear of a resurgence of enemy action. They beat the Arabs once, and could do it again!

The number of bookstores in Israel is extraordinary. Theatres and other cultural influences abound. In all, the observations of the 1949 traveler were to prove an omen of the vast development of the new State and its assured success in elevating the status of Jewry in every part of the world.

JEWS IN PRISON

BY CHAPLAIN ABRAHAM BURSTEIN

Jews in Prison

BY CHAPLAIN ABRAHAM BURSTEIN

ON NO MATTER of public interest is there so little knowledge or such imperfect knowledge as on that of prison life. With rare exceptions, the motion picture and popular book and newspaper provide completely wrongful impressions of correctional institutions. From rare insurrections in state penitentiaries, the average reader assumes that inmate and guard populations are in a constant state of armed peace or actual warfare.

Two extreme notions obsess most persons who at all ponder the punishment of malefactors. The first is that of the sob sister—the woman who weeps over the state of the poor unfortunates, and is sure that a little personal kindness on her part will bring about his virtually immediate rehabilitation. The worse the criminal, the more likely is one of these do-gooders to attempt to storm the prison door in his behalf.

The opposite notion is that all malefactors are the scum of the earth and must be treated with brutality compensatory of their sins against society. Oldtime guards used to work on that principle and consider themselves justified in inflicting additional physical punishment on their charges, generally surreptitiously.

In point of fact the prison inmate, unless definitely insane, is a completely normal person behind the walls. All persons sin; he has done something punishable and has been caught at it. It might surprise and discomfit the average citizen to learn that one out of eight or ten of the men he sees each day and perhaps does business with has at one time spent time in a punishment cell.

Another misconception, fostered largely by persons of radical political leanings and repeated unwittingly by many others, is that the characteristic prisoner has been jailed because he has

25

stolen a loaf of bread for his starving family. So far has the famed incident in "Les Misérables" entered into the thought of modern men. The truth is that were any such incident to occur in these days, the police themselves would help the family; and that in any case the percentage of crimes of larceny in prison population is no more than twenty. Despite the relief generally accorded the indigent in these days, such an idea persists in many minds.

The tendency toward limiting crime to some simple fact displays itself in the frequent remark to a newly met prison chaplain, "Oh, you take the condemned man on his last mile!" One must patiently explain that only one prison in a state, as a rule, carries out executions (Sing Sing in New York), and that even there the chaplain has little to do with the small number of condemned murderers. Over a period of years, the number of executions of Jews in Sing Sing has averaged one annually.

Despite all evidences to the contrary, also, protagonists of new social systems continue to rant that the changes they advocate will immediately reduce or obviate the commission of crime. Not alone has this not happened in the lands that have completely altered their social and governmental systems, but the invention of new crimes against the all-powerful state has increased the number of incarcerated by the millions. It must be understood that so long as there are acquisitiveness, sex, anger, and inbred deviltry among men they will violate the regulations established for the protection of the individuals and society among which they live.

All this must be comprehended before one ventures to study the circumstances involving any portion of the population, from the viewpoint of crime. It should be expected that Jews too are normal humans and are susceptible to breaking laws. They have the same impulse either to repeat the crime later or, as in four-fifths of all cases, to watch their conduct after a first offense. The differences reside in the comparative number of Jewish malefactors and in the influence of family ties on their normal conduct and their rehabilitation after apprehension in lawbreaking.

The eternal impulse of the non-Jew to judge all Jews by the evil actions of one can be grasped when one sees gentile readers perusing a frontpage report of a crime committed by a person with

a presumably Jewish name. I have answered such strictures by
suggesting that all the crime news in the paper be read and then
a percentage established. Or from my own position as senior
chaplain of the New York City Penitentiary, I can report conclusively that in every part of the country the number of Jews in
prison is far below their ratio of the population about them. In
this penitentiary, serving a population almost thirty percent
Jewish, the Jewish prisoners amount to approximately *three percent!* When the inmates are apprised of this fact, though they
themselves are in jail, they smile and applaud, rejoicing over the
rectitude of their coreligionists.

Another result of the long known family hold on the individual
Jew is the remarkably low rate of vagrancy among his people.
When in 1935 a roundup was made of ne'er-do-weels in New
York's Central Park, though every color and race and land of
origin seemed to be represented among the four hundred captives,
not one was a Jew. One can only refer to the Jewish laws that
declare that just as a man must rest on the Sabbath he must labor
on the other days, and that it is as important to feast before Yom
Kippur as it is to fast on the day itself. If a Jew is to go wrong, it
must not be through passive vagabondage but through some active
commission of wrongdoing.

The family cohesion of the Jew even in this disruptive period
is a source of wonder to prison officials. Rarely is the black sheep
entirely deserted, and even families that have been broken up for
many years are sometimes united in an effort to rebuild a home for
one who has strayed from society's fold as well as its own. I can my-
self report innumerable incidents of this nature, the most extraordinary of which concerns an eighty-year old mother whom an
inmate asked me to visit. The mother, after repeatedly denouncing
the son and wishing he were dead, and calling attention to other
sons who had achieved distinction in the community or died
gloriously in the war, as well as to the father who was unable to
survive his criminal son's disgrace, called me back as I was leaving,
and begged me to bring a small sum to her boy for his needs in
prison. The sum, gathered from drawers and beneath cloths,
amounted to a poor but glorious dollar and a half.

Sometimes a Jew who has died in prison is interred by a free burial society, but almost invariably a relative claims the body. The other side of the coin is evidenced by an old father who was found in the park, freezing, and was brought to the workhouse as a vagrant. Though he confided to a fellow inmate that he had four children who had refused to make a home for him, he resolutely refused to divulge their names as he was dying, lest any obloquy attach to the reputation of his own cruel children.

Anti-Semites, learning of the low percentage of Jewish prisoners, generally maintain in all seriousness that Jewish criminals escape punishment because they hire the best and most unscrupulous lawyers. The truth is that their lawyers, when they have any at all, are generally run-of-the-mill, and that a Jewish judge feels special anger against a fellow Jew who has sullied the name of his people, whereas the non-Jewish judge certainly will not favor the religious non-conformist before him. The plain fact is that the Jew is less criminal than his neighbors; that early training, family love, and pride of race are among the impulsions that keep him straight; and that even in prison he poses less of a problem to officers and chaplains than do other ethnic and religious groups.

WHY WE GET HEART DISEASE

BY JULIUS BURSTEIN, M.D.

Why We Get Heart Disease

BY JULIUS BURSTEIN, M.D.

THE HEART is a rugged muscular organ which pumps life's sustaining blood through the lungs and body. It can stand considerable abuse and takes no rest throughout life except between each individual pumping or contraction. The heart grows old and begins to wear out particularly in and after the fourth decade, and a seventy year old or older person may suffer from heart failure and death due to natural degenerative processes.

The two types of heart disease include congenital and acquired. Congenital heart disease is due to malformation in the embryonic growth of the heart. This may cause extraneous openings, malposition of the parts of the heart, obstructions in the course of the blood flow, and, in all but the mildest cases, inefficiency in the propulsion of the blood stream. Most people with congenital heart disease do not live out their full years. Congenital hearts are more prone to infection than normal hearts. In the past few years marvelous strides have been made in the surgical treatment of certain types of congenital heart disease. There is no known etiology for congenitally defective hearts. However, it has been observed that a relatively innocuous infection known as German measles, when occurring early in the mother's pregnancy, is prone to cause congenital defects in the baby's heart as well as in other parts of the body.

The second or acquired form of heart disease is the much more common type. In younger individuals infection involving the heart muscles and valves is the usual cause of heart trouble. In older people degenerative changes are more likely to occur in the heart. Very often we have a combination of both conditions, materially shortening a man's life.

The most common infection producing heart disease in the young is rheumatic fever. This illness causes inflammation of the heart muscles, valves, and linings, directly weakening the heart muscle as well as causing valvular defects. It may cause immediate death but, in most instances, leaves the heart in a crippled condition with shortened life expectancy. Other acute infections such as pneumonia, tonsillitis, diphtheria, scarlet fever, in fact all acute infections, will impair the heart muscles during the acute phase. Fortunately, in most instances, there is no marked permanent damage. It is understandable that, if the incidence of these acute infections is reduced by preventive medicine (immunization, prophylactic use of antibiotics, and hygienic measures), the infectious form of heart disease will be considerably reduced.

Rheumatic fever, the major heart crippler in the young, unfortunately has no specific cure. It is more common in the lower economic group where hygienic conditions are poor. Prevention of rheumatic fever, therefore, is a social as well as a medical problem. Some strides have been made in the treatment of acute attacks and a prevention of their recurrence by the use of various drugs, hormones, and antibiotics.

The most spectacular advances lately in the improvement of cases of chronic heart disease and cases of congenital heart abnormalities, have been in the field of cardiovascular surgery. Certain heart anomalies have been eliminated by surgery while others have shown considerable functional improvement under the same circumstances. Surgery of the heart, particularly where valvular defects are present, has improved the heart's mechanical efficiency and given increased life expectancy to a progressively larger number of heart invalids.

Heart disease from the fourth decade on is mostly of the chronic degenerative form. It is usually caused by changes in the arteries (arteriosclerosis) which become thickened, brittle, and of smaller lumen. When this process affects the blood vessels of the heart muscle itself, the coronary arteries, there is reduction and impairment of the blood flow to the heart. This curtailment of the blood supply over a long period of time leads to progressive degeneration of the heart muscle with concomitant reduction of heart efficiency.

This can lead to heart failure. Frequently a blood clot will form in one of these hardened arteries of the heart with a sudden stoppage of blood through that part of the heart muscle fed by that vessel (coronary thrombosis or occlusion). This results in sudden destruction of that part of the heart muscle (myocardial infarction). Death may result from this attack. However, the majority of the cases survive but with moderate to marked heart damage.

Longstanding high blood pressure which puts a permanent strain on the heart makes an individual more susceptible to coronary thrombosis. Patients with chronic diabetes are also more likely to have attacks involving the coronary (heart) arteries. Chronic illnesses as a whole seem to produce excessive arteriosclerosis and more frequent coronary attacks. Sometimes excessive physical exertion, overeating, or excitement will precipitate an attack of coronary occlusion. Syphilis has frequently caused trouble by scarring the openings of the coronary vessels.

Obesity, usually due to overeating, gives the heart more work to do directly. It also may cause fatty changes in the heart muscle. In a sense, therefore, this condition may be considered as a chronic cause of heart disease in older people. Tobacco smoking may cause abnormal cardiac rhythm and may also cause spasm of a coronary vessel. It must be included as a possible cause of heart disease in a susceptible individual.

In summation, we get heart disease because of faulty embryonic growth, acute infections in childhood, and degenerative changes in the blood vessels of the heart and in the heart itself in later years. The degenerative changes in the heart are apparently hastened by high blood pressure, various chronic illnesses, and bad habits of living. Although we may not be able to avoid heart disease in toto, we may be able to prevent the more serious consequences by living a regular life and being temperate in all our habits.

JUSTICE BENJAMIN N. CARDOZO

BY DR. MORRIS RAPHAEL COHEN

Justice Benjamin N. Cardozo

BY DR. MORRIS RAPHAEL COHEN

IT IS SIGNIFICANT that Justice Cardozo was one of the few of our judges who, like the late Justice Holmes, thought it important to *have* a philosophy. In the forefront of humanity's most cherished heroes, among prophets, saints, philosophers, scientists, poets, artists, and inspiring national leaders, the number of lawyers does not loom large. Mankind as a whole cannot well live by bread alone, but needs directing and sustaining vision, and it is hard for lawyers, bent on the affairs of the market place, to look up and see the heaven above. This is especially difficult in a country or epoch which, under the leadership of captains of industry and finance, worships a narrow practicality and acts as if theory can be safely ignored, if not despised. It requires, therefore, a high order of intellectual and moral energy for one who has been immersed almost all his life in the business of the law to avow and pursue an interest in its general background and ultimate outcome, following the maxim of the old talmudic sages that he who would deal justly with the law must contemplate the eternal issues of life and death. It is because Cardozo tried to do this that he became not only a great judge, rendering justice in the individual cases before him, but also a highly beloved national figure, inspiring Bench and Bar to a higher and more human conception of their duty to the community which they should serve.

The main features of Cardozo's, like those of any sound philosophy, are essentially simple, though it needs genius and energy to see their implications and to carry them out consistently. The first point is that law is not an isolated technique, of interest only to lawyers and to litigants, but that it is an essential part of the process of adjusting human relations in organized society. The second point is that the law of a growing society cannot all be contained in establishing precedents or any written documents, important as are continuity with the past and loyalty to the recorded will of the people. In the law as a social process, the judges play a determining role, having the sovereign power of choice in their decisions. It was in this emphasis on the judicial process that Cardozo's thought centered.

The third point, the logical corollary to the foregoing, is that to meet his responsibility for making the law serve human needs the judge cannot rely on legal authority alone, but must know the actual facts of the life about him, the psychologic and economic factors which determine its manifestations, and must thus keep abreast of the best available knowledge which those engaged in various social studies, researches, or investigations, can supply.

These three propositions are obvious, and they may even be said to have their roots in the old liberal faith which the founders of our Republic, men like Franklin, Jefferson, and James Wilson, held with fervor. But it requires vision and heroic courage to maintain this view today against the inertia and passionate errors of the prevalent attitude.

That law is and ought to be a closed, self-sufficient system, independent not only of the will but also of the social opinions of the judge, is one of those mischievous half or quarter truths which passes as an authoritative axiom among the unthinking. Its consequences may be illustrated by two actual incidents. At the banquet of one of our law schools a speaker took the legal profession to task because it was so much more interested in its own economic advancement than in eliminating the law's delays or helping the community to get justice more surely and more readily. Thereupon, the dean, a distinguished practitioner, replied with the eloquent rhetorical query, Why should we lawyers be called upon to act as social reformers? In another school after a case had been discussed and a student objected, "I don't see the justice of this decision," the professor answered, "This is a class in law, not in justice." Now there is of course some measure of truth in the latter contention. It is unfortunately true that many laws are unjust and are none the less part of our law. But from the historic and moral point of view this is surely not the final answer. The law arises to meet social needs and can maintain itself in the long run only if it serves those needs justly to the general satisfaction of the community. The Sabbath was made for man, and not man for the Sabbath.

The prevailing orthodoxy expressed some years ago by the late Senator Root and still passing as authoritative insists that the duty of the judge is simply to read and obey the statute or the Constitution and that it is no part of his business to make or change the law in any way. This assumes that the framers of a law or constitution can foresee all the possible future contingencies and make definite provisions for meeting them, so that the judge can be merely a logical automaton, a sort of phonograph repeating exactly what the law had definitely declared. But that has been characterized as childish by all great jurists. The effective meaning of such legal phrases as "due process" depends entirely on what the courts make it mean; and no student of history denies that when they stretched it to apply not only to legal processes or procedure but also to the substance of legislation, they gave it a meaning which it never had before the middle of the 19th century and still does not have in any other English or foreign court. Moreover, the basic assumption that general principles alone can determine individual decisions is one that all modern science has shown to be untenable. Legal principles may supply guiding analogies, but the decision of any individual case depends on an understanding of the actual social conditions, and of the consequences of the decision, as well as on the judge's view as to which of these consequences are best. Now elevation to the bench does not make a man omniscient, and the obvious fiction that courts decide only points at law prevents us from giving them adequate facilities for investigation into the relevant facts of the case, and into the larger social consequences of their decisions. In our anxiety to make judges independent of the popular will we are making them independent of the knowledge necessary to make their work satisfactory.

Philosophic wisdom, or spiritual insight, shows itself in genuine humility, and it is the genuine humility of Justice Cardozo that made him realize that to do his work justly and adequately he needed more light than mere precedents or the usual legal authorities. Not only is law connected with other phases of human life, but as social conditions are changing the meaning or bearing of law or legal principles must change accordingly. Economic maxims formulated generations ago can no longer be relied on today. They must be corrected by more recent information. Absolute knowledge or infallibility is not given to human beings in dealing with human affairs, and a conscientious judge must keep abreast and avail himself of all the contributions in the various fields of social study. Cardozo was, indeed, criticized for quoting non-legal authorities in some of his judicial opinions. But such pleas for ignorance come too late. History has too often shown the fine fruits for science and civilization in the marriage of thought to fact.

Every genuine philosophy reflects not only one's personality but is conditioned by one's life experience. It should be a source of pride that our country still offers opportunity for the development of real merit such as Cardozo's, regardless of his unorthodox creed. But it should be more than a matter of pride. At a time when there is real danger of the world reverting to the medieval barbaric view in which men are judged entirely by their tribal descent and conformity to prevailing orthodoxy, there is an inescapable duty on all of us to maintain this liberal faith with all our might. And to do this it is well to keep green in our national memory the lives and teachings of spiritual heroes like Benjamin Nathan Cardozo.

THE CALLING OF THE JEWS

BY DR. ALBERT EINSTEIN

The Calling of the Jews

BY DR. ALBERT EINSTEIN

THIS IS A TIME when there seems to be a particular need for men of philosophical persuasion—that is to say, friends of wisdom and truth—to join together. For it is true that our time has accumulated more knowledge than any earlier age, that love of truth and insight which lent wings to the spirit of the Renaissance has grown cold, giving way to sober specialization rooted in the material spheres of society rather than in the spiritual. But groups such as this one are devoted solely to spiritual aims.

In centuries past Judaism clung exclusively to its moral and spiritual tradition. Its teachers were its only leaders. But with adaptation to a larger social whole this spiritual orientation has receded into the background, even though today the Jewish people owe to it their apparently indestructible vigor. If we are to preserve that vigor for the benefit of mankind, we must hold to that spiritual orientation toward life.

The dance about the Golden Calf was not merely an episode in the history of our forefathers—an episode that seems to me in its simplicity more innocent than that total adherence to material and selfish goals threatening Judaism in our own days. At this time a union of those who rally to the spiritual heritage of our people has supreme justification. This is all the more true for a group that is free of all historical and national narrowness. We Jews should remain the carriers and patrons of spiritual values. But we should also always be aware of the fact that these spiritual values have been increasingly accepted as the common goal of all mankind.

TRIBUTE TO PROF. ISRAEL DAVIDSON

BY DR. ISMAR ELBOGEN

Tribute to Prof. Israel Davidson

BY DR. ISMAR ELBOGEN

THE DEATH of Israel Davidson, which occurred on June 27, 1939, in the 69th year of his life, deprived American Israel of an outstanding scholar and a great man, and those who were close to him of a true and loyal friend. Little can be added to the admirable eulogy which Dr. Louis Finkelstein, provost and professor of the Jewish Theological Seminary of America, published in the recent issue of the American Jewish Year Book.

We need not dwell on the hardships of Dr. Davidson's youth and early manhood, and on the heroic struggle which culminated in his becoming a doctor of philosophy at Columbia University (1902), professor at the Jewish Theological Seminary (1905), honorary doctor of several learned institutions, honorary fellow of our Academy, and author of momentous contributions to Jewish scholarship.

Dr. Davidson specialized in Hebrew poetry, and most of his numerous publications cover this field. His first volume, "Parody in Jewish Literature" (1907), was a comprehensive presentation of one section of this poetry, not the usual thesis, but an extremely learned book which draws an enormous amount of material from manuscripts and rare works, and offers a thorough idea of all branches of parody in medieval Hebrew lore. He himself had a fine sense of humor, loved a good jest, and felt congenial in this field of literature.

He enlarged his studies to embrace Hebrew poetry in general, and enriched this long neglected study by remarkable publications, of which only a few outstanding ones can here be mentioned. The widest known is his "Selected Poems of Solomon ibn Gabirol," with Israel Zangwill's translation and Davidson's elucidation of Gabirol's place in poetry—published in the Schiff Jewish Classics Series (1923).

Two of his works will render his name immortal—his "Mahzor Yannai," published in 1919, and his "Thesaurus of Medieval Hebrew Poetry" אוצר השירה והפיוט —of which the first volume appeared in 1924 and the fourth in 1933. Yannai is the name of one of his earliest liturgical poets, but nothing was known about him. One of his hymns is most popular because it was inserted in the Passover Hagadah— ובכן ויהי בחצי חלילה —but unfortunately the name of the poet was not disclosed, and only a century ago it was discovered that this was one section of a composition by Yannai. That was all. The Jewish Encyclopedia contained a facsimile of a fragment of Aquila's Greek translation of the Bible; but as the Jews of later ages had no use for Greek, they wrote Hebrew poetry over that particular parchment. Many of us saw this palimpsest, but none took the trouble to examine the Hebrew text. Dr. Davidson did—and his was the important discovery that the Hebrew writ contained fragments of compositions by Yannai. Thereafter he discovered more of them, and in a small book he presented full evidence that Yannai had been a most prolific poet, and had composed poetical readings in accordance with the Triennial Cycle. That meant not less than 155 such compositions, not to speak of his illustrations of all the festivals. Davidson's was pioneer work. Other students found more and more of Yannai's poetry; and in 1938 we beheld an entire volume of Piyyute Yannai, restoring nearly two thirds of the poet's work. Dr. Davidson was happy to review this publication—the successful growth of his seed.

A far greater achievement is his Thesaurus. Hebrew poetry had shared the fate of the Jewish people; it was, if possible, even more scattered, even more crippled. None could find their way through that almost impervious literary diaspora. But Israel Davidson attempted to bring order into this chaos. Through years of indefatigable labor he collected all the available printed Hebrew poetry, composed from early post-biblical times to the year 1740— some forty thousand items, secular as well as religious. He then published their first lines in alphabetical order—adding the source where each poem was to be found, how each was printed, whether it had been translated into other languages, and where it was discussed in the literature. To better known selections, particularly old prayers, he added a critical analysis and appreciation. The fourth volume not only presents rich additional material, made accessible to Prof. Davidson during his stay in Palestine and Egypt, but also made a list of the numerous authors, with cross reference to their already mentioned poems. Davidson's Thesaurus is a standard work. No one can write on Hebrew poetry without continuously consulting and quoting this treasury, which never fails the student. Well aware of the importance of this work, Dr. Davidson was eager to keep it up to date by continuous supplements of recent publications. Of these one was printed and another prepared for print; it is to be hoped that in the interest of Jewish scholarship others will see that the series be continued.

Dr. Davidson's last years were dedicated to editing the poetical section of the Siddur of Saadia. Saadia Gaon (died 942) was the pioneer of individual and systematic Jewish literature, but most of his works have been lost. Davidson discovered part of his polemical writings, and was glad to share in the publication of this oldest of all Jewish prayer books—which, though promised several times during the past fifty years, had never been achieved. His materials are so well prepared that were they not handicapped by war conditions, his coeditors in Jerusalem could at once complete the volume.

This was not the only manuscript which our lamented friend was not able to see printed. He left quite a number of them. It is amazing what a huge mass of work this devoted student, who was a sick man for many years, had in mind to complete. There are several volumes of the poetry of the famed Israel Nadjara thesaurus, an uncollated collection of Hebrew proverbs covering more than 1200 years, awaiting a redactor and publisher. It is highly desirable that American Jewry find a redeemer for these waiting works.

In his last will Israel Davidson advised us not to mourn his death. He could rightly expect that his name would live so long as Hebrew poetry is studied. But irreparable is the loss of his charming personality. All of us who knew him will never forget him.

PSYCHIATRIC CONCEPTS IN BIBLE, TALMUD AND ZOHAR

BY HIRSCH LOEB GORDON, PH.D., M. D., F. A. P. A.

Psychiatric Concepts
in Bible, Talmud and Zohar

BY HIRSCH LOEB GORDON, PH.D., M.D., F.A.P.A.

JUDAISM has always been concerned with the emotions. They were even allegorically ascribed to the Almighty, both in the Bible and in Talmud and Midrash. Of the approximately six thousand word-roots found in the old Hebrew language the greater part express human feelings and moods, from joy to sorrow, from ecstasy to gloom. The lyrical supplications of the Psalmist who laments over his destiny and demands protection and vengeance, the wail of Jermiah in Echah over the national catastrophe that befell Israel, the unconsolable grief of Job and the exhortations of the prophets are replete with passion. Human conduct in all of its shades and degrees are praised or censured by the prophets and the wise Solomon while the Song of Songs echoed the pangs of frustated lovers' infatuation. In their poetic imagery the authors of the Holy Writ made the chambers of the heart, kidneys, liver, guts, hips, bosom, knees, bones, and other organs vehicles for all human experience. But it was the spirit *(ruah)* and the soul *(nefesh, neshamah)*, all related to the breath of life and used interchangeably (Job 12:10; 34:14), that represented the entire human personality, his total individuality.

Psychiatry studies the behavior and treatment of the mentally ill. Psychology studies the behavior of the mentally normal. It is universally accepted that in a mental disease the patient's acts, thoughts, or feelings are greatly influenced by the character traits of his previous so-called "pre-psychotic" personality, which are now either exaggerated, deviated from the normal, or altered to their opposite mirror-image, in accordance with the law of opposites in modern dynamic psychiatry. It is worth studying some of the biblical and talmudical assumptions of normal human behavior when the law is involved.

Such assumptions, in the form of brief proverbial statements, are encountered in myriads throughout the *Halachah* (Law), and guide its legal decisions. Jewish jurisprudence thus appears not as a formal collection of rigid, inflexible unconditionally applicable ordinances, but as a principle of justice and fairness that takes into consideration not only unforeseen and exceptional situations, but also the behavior of people in conformity with the individual's specific qualities of reaction.

The *"Umdana"* (conjecture) was applied in estimating the true intentions of a person acting under stress (B. Batra 146b). Wrongdoing under *"Ones"* (compulsion, duress) was "exonerated by the Merciful One" (*Sifre, Ki teze*) and a failure to comply with a legal demand is thus remitted (Ned. 27a), although in the case of rape an opinion is expressed that the initial moral resentment may gradually turn into an inward, instinctual consent (Ket. 51b).

The normal individual is assumed not to make a meaningless statement (Arachin 5); not purposely to leave his heirs in predicament (Shabuot 47a); to accept an act that benefits him though he was not previously consulted about it (Erubin 81b); not to allow a stranger to use his property unless he has sold it or rented it to him (Tos. Ked. 1, 2); to be assumed alive (in the normal span of life) unless there is information to the contrary (Holin 11a). Also if he be a commissioned agent he fulfills his task (Er. 31b); is not insolent when facing his creditors (B. Kama 107a); does not toil for nothing (Jeb. 107a); does not anticipate the return of a lost article devoid of identifying marks or after the lapse of a certain time (B. Mezia 21b); does not lie while talking nonchalantly, unaware of legal implications (Gitt. 28b); does neither lie (Jerus. B. Mezia, 1) nor jest on his death-bed (B. Batra 175a); does not admit his guilt (Sab. 119a); can not absolutely prevent unchastity (Ket. 13b); does not benefit from crime (Sheviit 9, 9); does not like members of his own profession (Gen. R. 32, 2).

That emotional sufferings are as grave as physical afflictions has been shown in the Pentateuch in the two portions (Leviticus XXVI and Deuteronomy XXVIII) in which the children of Israel were forewarned of the calamities awaiting them if they would not hearken to the Lord, but spurn his statutes, and break his covenant. These lists imply that they are calculated to produce a more crushing effect than the physical castigations preceding them.

The Levitical list of "Curses" begins with "consumption, fever that causes life to pine away . . . to be smitten before enemies . . . broken pride of power . . . invasion by wild beasts . . . sword of vengeance . . . famine that will make cannibalism compulsory . . . cities laid waste . . . dispersion in strange lands . . . " and reaches its climax in "faintness of heart . . . turning to flight at the sound of a driven leaf . . . flight as from a sword where none pursues."

The list in Deuteronomy XXVIII also proceeds from maladies of the body to the mind, the latter being: "confusion, failure, be example of horror . . . madness, blindness, and astonishment of heart, groping at noonday as the blind grope in darkness . . . lack of success. Be oppressed and robbed with no one to help . . . Maddening sights . . . no ease, no rest . . . a trembling heart, failing eyes, languishing soul . . . insecurity, suspended life . . . day and night terror . . . doubt in one's own life" (66) . We have in these impressive descriptions states of mind which are known now as vexations, continuous doubts, startle reactions, hysterias, feelings of inferiority, paranoid states, anticipations of impending disaster, agitated depressions, illusions, auditory and visual hallucinations.

Psychiatry, like medicine and other scientific and social disciplines, appear to us in the Bible, Talmud, and Codes not as independent objects of study, but only in connection with the Law; in other words, as means to regulate human relations in the spirit of justice and kindness. The Jewish Law has always accepted the psychological approach to human nature in all its shades of strength and weakness.

The inherent "animal" nature of man was pointed out by the Lord Himself when He declared after the Flood: "For the nature (*Yezer*) of the heart of man is evil from his youth." And Zophar,

Job's friend, declared: "A man is born a wild ass's colt" (Job 11, 12). Ecclesiastes added: "The preeminence of man over beast is nought" (3, 19). The idea that the soul oscillates between the driving powers of the "Evil nature" (*Yezer Ra*) and "good nature" (*Yezer Tov*) (Berachot 61a) appears to be the pattern for Freud's psychical organization of the personality into the central *Ego,* the instinctual *Id,* and the inhibiting, moralizing, standard-setting *Super-Ego.* The relationship, I would even say, the borrowing of these concepts, is even more striking, when we note in the Talmud that the Id (*Yezer Ra*) is with man at birth (Sanhedrin 91b), and that the Super-Ego is a product of later development, under the influence of parents, teachers, and high social ideals; as the Midrash expresses it, "It joins man at the age of thirteen" (Koheleth R., 4, 9; Abot Der. Nathan, 16). Freud does not consider the subconscious instincts of the Id as specifically evil when they satisfy innate needs, nor does the Midrash: "If not for the *Yezer Ra* man would not have bought a house, taken a woman into marriage, caused children to be born, and engaged in commerce" (Ber. R., 9) ; and the Talmud: "Let us be grateful to our ancestors, for it they had not succumbed to instinctual desires (sex-urges) we would not have arrived into this world" (Abodah Zarah, 5A). As the Id is a partner in the conflict between instinctual cravings and their inhibitions by higher ideals (Super-Ego), both Freud and the Midrash agree that an animal has no *Yezer Ra* (Aboth de R. Nathan 16).

Competence to perform a legal act and responsibility for crime presuppose a normal mind. The feeble-minded, psychoneurotic, psychopathic and psychotic are usually exonerated by our criminal law, if the mental derangement has made it unable for the offender to form a criminal intent and rendered him incapable of distinguishing between right and wrong.

Resh Lakish, who is the author of profound observations in the field of mental diseases, said: "A man does not commit a sin unless the spirit of insanity (*shetut*) has entered into him" Sotah 3A).

The Beraita gave the first basic description of insanity: "Who is insane? The one who walks alone at night and who stays overnight in a cemetery, and rends apart his garments" (Hagigah 3, 2) . The Gemara adds: "One who loses everything given to him" (Hagigah 4a) .

As a practicing psychiatrist, whenever I feel forced to send a patient to a mental institution in order to protect him or society or both from probable harm, and I must give the ambulance driver a note to assure that the admitting physician see the necessity of hospitalization, I can safely open the treatise Hagigah and convert the beautifully expressed symptoms into modern prosaic verbiage: "This patient is seclusive, destructive, and cannot take care of himself."

Maimonides, who was not only the greatest physician of his time, but also a profound psychological observer, elaborated the Beraita's definitions and, as though writing in our times, widened the frame of abnormal behavior by including many less pronounced traits, when he ruled (in connection with the competence to bear witness in court) : "Insane (*Shoteh*) is considered not only one who walks around nude, breaks things, and casts stones, but who suffers confusion of the mind and whose reasoning is erroneous in any aspect, even though his inquiries and responses are relevant in other things . . . An epileptic is considered incompetent during his seizure but competent at other times. There are, however, epileptics who even during their seizure-free periods are confused. The mentally defective who fail to identify things, who are contradictory in their statements, and have less understanding than the uneducated, and also those who are agitated and impulsive and those who behave abnormally, may be considered as insane."

The deaf, the insane, and minors are not considered legally competent and are not responsible for their acts. As to the deaf, opinions differ; some believe that deafness alone is disqualifying, others that it must be accompanied by muteness (Edut, 9, 9-11) .

The problem of juvenile delinquency occupies an important part in Mosaic legislation (Deut. 21:18-21) . A delinquent is called: "A deviating and spiteful son," who persists in his bad habits even after he is punished by his parents. He is then tried by the elders of the city as a glutton and a drunkard, and if found guilty is stoned to "purge evil from your midst" (Deut. 21:22).

The fate of a juvenile delinquent was in reality not as harsh as appears on the surface. Maimonides (Chapter "Mamrim") summarized the specific conditions under which capital punishment was meted out to him. He is liable for punishment only during three months of his life, following the appearance of the first two pubic hairs. He must steal money from his father, indulge in gluttony (of cattle meat only), and inebriety (in wine only), in the company of hoodlums. He must be of normal sexual development, and of normal parents, both of whom must be living and agree to surrender him to the judges. The parents had the right to forgive him before the judges' decision was given. Because of these stringent requirements Simeon Ben Gamaliel declared: There was never and will never be a case of a "deviated and spiteful" son (Sanh. 71a). But their concern with unchecked criminal tendencies in juveniles may be gathered from the statement: "This boy who regularly indulges in pleasures without working, will ultimately, having used up his father's money, turn out a highway robber" Sanh. 72a).

The Talmud considered sociability one of the most desirable human traits, as antidote to the malignancy of seclusive existence. This is illustrated by the saying: "A person must not exclude himself from the community" (Berachot 49b); "Do not stay away from human society" (Abot 2, 4); "Either companionship or death!" (Taanit 23a).

The concept of psychosomatics is not missing from Jewish traditional literature. "When Satan suggested to the Lord: 'Hurt his bone and flesh,' and the Lord answered: 'Here he is in your hand, but protect his life' (Job 1:5-6), the latter experienced more pain than Job. He had to break the barrel without spilling its wine" (B. Batra 16a).

That a skin rash breaks out as punishment for evil gossip, (Arachin 16a, Deut. R. 6) is based on what happened to Miriam after she spoke disparagingly about her brother Moses for having married an Ethiopian woman (Num. 12:1, 10). This opinion was shared by Maimonides (Tumeat Zoraath, 16).

It is remarkable that according to present psychosomatic medicine certain skin diseases are provoked by repressed hostility towards a parent or closely related person, and also as an erotic capitalization of suffering in self-punishment. K. A. Menninger and N. W. Ackerman have cited such cases.

A remarkable utilization of emotional shock in surgery is related in Holin 56a:

"An Aramean saw a man falling off a roof to the ground and [also noted] that his abdomen burst open, throwing his intestines outside. He brought the son [of the wounded man] before him and made believe that he had slaughtered him. The wounded man was shocked, sighed deeply, and drew in his prolapsed guts, after which the abdomen was sutured." The clever emergency surgeon, who may have been a layman, thus utilized human stress emotions to replace the abdominal contents without the use of his hands.

During my service in the Medical Corps of the U. S. Army I was amazed at the large number of enlisted men who suffered a nervous breakdown at the very beginning of their army life, and who were never sent overseas. In reviewing their life histories through childhood, adolescence and early adulthood, interviewing parents who came to visit them, I noted how dependent these boys were on their overprotective fathers and mothers, and that they formed no heterosexual relations. In other words, they were immature, and consequently were guided not by reality, but by wishes, fears, and fantasies. They could not do their own thinking, make their own decisions, or assume responsibilities. In fact, they even lacked the capacity to love some one other than themselves. They were dependent but not dependable. I then recalled that these emotional casualties could not adjust to the normal personality adaptations of adolescence as expressed early in the Bible about normal young men capable of reaching adulthood and starting a life of their own: "Therefore a man *leaves* his father and his mother and cleaves to his wife and they become one flesh" (Gen. 2:24).

Dreams occupy an eminent role in psychoanalytic thinking. According to Freud dreams are assumed to be a form of communication from the unconscious part of the mind. They are a disguised fulfillment of suppressed wishes. According to Adler a dream foreshadows the preparations developed in connection with actual difficulties encountered by the dreamer's lifeplan. It warns and encourages. The essence of dreams is often absurdity, incoherence, and senselessness. Many dreams are ambiguous. Their contents are symbolic.

The persecuted, frightened, fleeing Jacob, forced to leave his native land and threatened with violence by his brother Esau, subconsciously produced the "ladder dream" at Beth El, in which the Lord promised to be with him, to protect him, to return him to the land and give him possession of it (Gen. 28:12-15). The daring ambitions of Joseph found expression in his dreams of the sheaves which bowed to *his* sheaf, and the sun, moon and eleven stars which bowed down to him (Gen. 37). The dreams of Pharaoh, who knew of the famines that had befallen his country in the past, could foresee such later tragedies, symbolized by cows and ears of corn. The divine warning dreams of Abimelech (Gen. 20:1-18), Laban (31:24), and Balaam (Nu. 22:23) could also be interpreted psychiatrically, that God had transmitted them through the voice of the Super-Ego from the unconscious. However, leaving alone the prophetic nocturnal visions of the few chosen ones, we may safely state that in evaluation of dreams of the average man, woman, and child, Bible, Talmud, and psychiatry are in harmony. Their mystic significance has been denied in the statements of the prophet Zechariah: "And dreams speak what is false" (10,2). The Talmud also declares: "Items of dreams neither promote nor degrade" (an idiomatic expression for "valueless") (San. 30a). "No dream is devoid of worthless items." "A man is shown what his heart reflects" (Ber. 55a). "King David never saw a good dream. All his days he was busy in shedding blood and leading battles, so that all his dreams were bad ones, of ruin and of devastation" (Zohar, Mikez).

The bad effect of a terrifying dream was removed by the great amora and physician, Samuel, who would cite Zechariah: "And dreams speak what is false". They stated further that "All dreams follow the mouth" (Ber. 55c), namely, as they are interpreted so they are (Ber. 56a). And therefore the Rabbis instituted a "Dream Solving" (*pitron halomoth*) procedure. The anxious dreamer faces three of his friends, to whom he says seven times: "I saw a *good* dream"—to which they reply seven times: "You saw a *good* dream. It is good and wil be good. The good God will make it good. Heaven will proclaim seven times that it will be good." A special prayer for the favorable significance of dreams was instituted to be recited in the synagogue during the blessings of the priests (Ber. 62.). There were professional "Dream Interpreters," but they were not always in agreement, as their purpose was to convert unpleasant details to well-meaning omens. And R. Banaah said: "24 dream interpreters were in Jerusalem. Once I dreamt a dream and went to all of them. Each one of them gave me a different interpretation and all of those interpretations were realized in my life" (Ber. 56a). The Rabbis even practiced experimental dreams. King Sapor (the First, 227-40, c.e) of Neo-Persia, said to his friend Samuel: "You claim to be wise men. If so, can you foretell what I will dream tonight? And Samuel answered: You will dream that the Romans conquered your land, took you prisoner, and ground for you kernels of dates in golden millstones. The king thought so much about it that he dreamt of it that night" (Ber. 56a).

The virtue of optimism has been greatly extolled: "God resides in man only when he is happy" (Ber. 31a). "My son, if you can afford it, be good to yourself, as there is no delight in hell and death is not slow in arriving" (Erubin 4a). "O, sharp-minded one: make haste and eat, make haste and drink, because the world we are departing from is like a feast house" (Idem). "A man will be tried for not eating things that he saw" (Jerus. Kiddushin, end). "Whoever fasts (for private reasons) is named a sinner" (Taan. 11a). "Whoever can afford to eat barley and eats wheat bread commits the sin of malice towards oneself" (Sabbath 140b).

As a self assuring phrase in times of stress, there is none better than that used by the unfortunate Nahum of Gimzo: he was totally blind, without arms and legs, and his entire body was covered with boils. Yet he said, as affliction followed affliction: "This too, is for the good" (Taanith 21a). One can now understand why R. Akiba, the greatest of all teachers of the Talmud, went to him for instruction. Under the terrible persecution of Emperor Hadrian, during which time Akiba himself met a martyr's death, Nahum's optimistic dictum helped Israel to survive.

The Bible and the Talmud contain also the principles of modern psychiatric therapy. We must recall at the very beginning the almost prophetic statement of the sagacious Resh Lakish of 1600 years ago: "Insanity—we have no medication for it in our hands" (Gittin 70b). If modern physicians would heed the statement of Resh Lakish and cease trying to cure the mentally ill with "medication" (sedatives, sleeping pills, vitamins, hematinics, and hormones) and refer them early to psychiatrists—many tragedies could be averted, many lives saved.

Psychoanalytic Therapy

In psychoanalytic therapy the patient states in the presence of his psychiatrist every thing that comes to his mind by the process of free association. It is not a form of question and answer. This last is unreliable even from the viewpoint of the Talmud: "A man does not declare himself wicked" (Jeb. 25b). "A man cannot see himself culpable" (Sab. 119a). It is only when one "chatters with innocence" (*Lefi Tumo*), making statements unaware of their possible implications, that he is most reliable (Jeb. 121b).

The book of proverbs has already advised: "When anxiety is in the heart of man, let him *talk it out*" (12, 25). Job made a request: "Keep silence toward me that I may speak, and something will pass away from me" (13,13). Elijah, his friend, declared: "I must speak, that I may find relief" (Job 32, 20). Joseph knew very well the therapeutic value of removing from memory worry and nostalgia when he called his son *Menasseh* (he makes one to forget), for "God has made me forget all my hardship and all my father's house" (Gen. 41, 51).

Many rituals were established by the Rabbis based on their knowledge of human anxieties. Thus, in the Grace after meals, to relieve the Jew of his worries during eating and to assist the digestive process, they included such calming phrases as: "We shall never be without food . . . He will break the yoke of dispersion and lead us upright to our land . . . They will justify us in heaven and make us worthy to live to the days of Messiah's coming."

The "Reading of Shema" prayer before retiring also contains many reassurances of great value to those who cannot relax and fall asleep because of fears. It begins with a kind of self-hypnosis when one declares himself already somnolent, thanking God "who makes the bands of sleep to fall on my eyes and slumber on my eyelids." One must consider God near, his invisibility notwithstanding. "The Most High dwells in secrecy. He shall cover you with his pinion and under his wing you will find shelter." Even with terrifying sounds and sights of the night, "of pestilence that stalks in darkness—no evil shall befall you . . . The angels will be commanded to protect you . . . Upon their hands they will bear you . . . To my right is archangel Michael, and my left archangel Gabriel, and facing me is archangel Uriel; behind me is archangel Raphael, and over my head is the Presence of God."

PRESENTATION OF HON. BENJAMIN N. CARDOZO

BY LEON HUHNER

Presentation of
Hon. Benjamin N. Cardozo

BY LEON HUHNER

IT IS A GREAT PRIVILEGE, and to me a source of pleasure and pride, to present for Honorary Fellowship in this Academy the name of one who ranks among the foremost men of our time, a great judge, a brilliant jurist and philosopher, a splendid citizen and a sterling American, the Hon. Benjamin Nathan Cardozo, one of the Justices of the Supreme Court of the United States.

We, as Jews, feel a just pride in the exalted position he has attained, not only because of his rare gifts, but because he has always lived up to the highest standards of honor and integrity.

Mr. Justice Cardozo is descended from an old Spanish and Portuguese family which settled in America long before the War of Independence. Among his ancestors were men enrolled on the patriot side during the Revolution, and among his kin was the Rev. Gershom Mendes Seixas, the patriot Minister of Shearith Israel of this City, who closed the doors of the synagogue on the advent of the British rather than continue under the enemy's auspices. The Rev. Mr. Seixas was among the first to return after the evacuation of the City and later became one of the incorporators of Columbia College, whose Trustee he remained for many years.

By ancestry and sentiment, therefore, Mr. Justice Cardozo is bound to New York where he was born in 1870. He was educated at Columbia and has served on its Board of Trustees. He was admitted to the bar in 1891, and from the very start, has been looked upon as an ornament of the profession and was esteemed a leader at the bar, long before his elevation to the Bench. In 1914 he was designated to serve as a Judge of the New York Court of Appeals, of which he later became Chief Judge. His career in that great court brought him signal recognition not only in his State, but throughout the entire country, so that when Mr. Justice Holmes resigned from the U. S. Supreme Court, Judge Cardozo's name naturally suggested itself to the American Bar and to the President of the United States to succeed to that exalted position.

The general acclaim of his nomination by the American press, irrespective of political affiliation, showed the great esteem in which he was held. His decisions in the N. Y. Court of Appeals and since then in the highest tribunal of the land have attracted the attention of jurists and statesmen everywhere, not only for their fairness and lucidity, but for their originality of reasoning and the truly philosophical outlook at their basis.

Honors have come thick and fast to this distinguished man, who holds the highest academic degrees from Columbia, Yale, Harvard, and from many other great seats of learning.

As an author quite aside from his admirable decisions, his contributions, particularly to the philosophy of law, have been acclaimed again and again.

But despite all the great honors which have come to him, Justice Cardozo has never for a moment forgotten that he is a Jew, and his wise counsel has ever been at the service of our people, whenever he was called upon.

Any great institution which cultivates the arts and sciences and cherishes scholarships, would deem it an honor to have the name of Justice Cardozo upon its rolls, and it is with pride and pleasure therefore, that I present his name as an Honorary Fellow to this Academy.

THREE DILEMMAS ABOUT GOD AND MAN

BY REV. DR. LEO JUNG

Three Dilemmas
About God and Man

BY REV. DR. LEO JUNG

Introduction

WHEN THE ARABS took over the pre-occupation with speculative philosophy which for hundreds of years had been characteristic of the Greeks, they added to its scope as they began to link it with the theological problems which had agitated their scholars in the isolated academies of their faith. One of the questions they bequeathed to the Jews touched upon the limits of omnipotence. Could God perform the impossible? No, was their answer: God's omnipotence extends to all things, but the impossible is a nothing, hence the question is self-canceled. Saadya,[1] Rambam,[2] Crescas,[3] were wrestling with, and finally endorsed, their solution.

Consistently, neither they nor we would fitly ascribe dilemmas to God. Our thought, Maimonides has shown, is not only quantitatively, but especially qualitatively, different from God's: *lo mahshevotai mahshevotekhem*,[4] "My thoughts are not your thoughts," as Isaiah put it. But, transferring the principle of *dibrah Torah bileshon bene Adam*,[5] "The Torah speaks in the language of man," to the consideration of intellectual problems, we recognize certain conflicting thoughts in our formulation of divine policies as far as we can reconstruct them from definite statements, occasional allusions, and deep mysteries of theosophic language. Our present concern is not with the timeworn school-questions of God's Prescience versus man's Freedom of Will, but with some important tangential matters. Three such "dilemmas" are to be briefly discussed here, because positing them may somewhat aid our attempt to escape from the labyrinth of theodicy, the attempt to justify the ways of God to man as far as the starting-point, the road and the goal are intelligible or visible to us. They are:

71

I. Freedom of Will and Escape by the Skin of our Teeth.
II. The Quest for Knowledge and the Resignation off the Goal.
III. Rewards and Punishments, and the Safety Margin for an Ethical Personality.

* * *

I. Freedom of Will and Escape by the Skin of our Teeth

Without freedom of will we would be reduced to automata, concerning whom the terms efficient or non-efficient might be apposite, but who could not be performing good or evil deeds. Minus freedom of will there is no intelligent choice, indeed, no choice at all. Whether we are pessimistically inclined to reduce that freedom to a minimum, allowing environmental influence the major chance, and granting but a narrow margin to the exercise of our own judgment: or even if we lightheartedly presume to ignore the pressure of *mores* and temporal powers, allowing a maximum power for our deliberation, decision, and action thereupon—ethical thinking in particular, as religious theory in general, takes an irreducible chance for human choice for granted. For, unless we are convinced that every man has freedom to choose, we cannot call him wise or foolish. For his choice to deserve either value judgment, he must have been free to decide between alternatives. On the same basis, and on that alone, can his *action* be termed either good or bad. All religion, as it promises reward or threatens punishment, must postulate such freedom. No matter how we refine reward, whether as material goods, health, happiness, prosperity, wealth, honor, dignity, the fulfillment of basic desires like food, drink, love, shelter, or of satisfaction on a higher level, such as a clear conscience, saturation with noble self-consciousness, the awareness of unity with cosmic right, harmony, ethical perfection; no matter how we imagine punishment: in terms of hell-fire, public censure, or the torments of a guilty conscience; in the frame of Lucas von Cranach or in the scenes of de Rivera, either contingency is conditioned by the belief in man as a free agent, influenced, perchance or more assuredly by outside forces, but definitely granted an ultimate authority of decision between one of two roads, both of which are open to him.

The Torah does not discuss freedom of will. Its legislation is based on that assumption. But it also states explicitly:[6] *"I place before you this day blessing and curse, life and death; choose thou life."* Every son of man, however, can, if he wishes to, choose death. That makes his choosing life wise and good. Every human can advance, within his sphere of action and influence, the cause of good. Every human being can and will do evil. The sages in the Talmud indicate that[7] any evil *intention,* even if unattended by acts, by a deed expressing it, is evil; that punishment is entailed when the evil intention is realized by an act; that good intention, even if unattended by its success, is good and merits reward.

The generations of the flood were destroyed because they abused their freedom of will by wreaking their oppressive will upon the weaker elements in their community. Abraham was accorded praise for deciding to accept the Lord's promise in spite of the testimony of his experience which seemed to contradict it. Because he believed in[8] (lit., *"made true" by his act of faith, he-emin*) the unlikely but not impossible arrival of an heir at that late date in his own and his wife's life; because he believed in (and thus made true) his victory over Chedorlaomer, arrogant enslaver of the five little kings; because he overthrew all contemporary *mores* by his refusal to accept payment[9] for his crusade on behalf of the weaker vessels, he was adjudged meritorious. All these and countless other cases mentioned between Genesis XII and the end of the Second Book of Chronicles exemplify and re-emphasize the Bible's position: God grants man freedom of will and holds him accountable for its use or abuse.

But two difficulties arise: One is implied in the Lord's premise never again to destroy the world by flood (or anything else, as the commentaries have it), which means, to temper justice with mercy. This would seem to discourage a right choice by suggesting an escape to evildoers. Man's conscience, indeed, may be viewed as a check on his headlong rush towards evil. "The still, small voice" does present the claim of right, the reaction to greed and other selfishness. Whether conscience be viewed as an emotion or as an authoritative judgment—all the nuances of opinion from Butler[10] and Kant[11] to T. V. Smith[12]—it may impress man's imagination, deflect his passionate energies, and thus serve as God's ambassador, before the court of man's will. But conscience does not penetrate the pachydermosity of the robust egoist, nor remove the iron curtain of fanaticism. It functions neither always, nor with all the people. It would allow human beings margins of disastrous possibilities.

Hence, the other practical necessity and moral problem: To prevent man from running amok to the extent that by violence, selfishness, or folly, he ruin the world in which by wise choice of action he could achieve the permanence of a classless, warless society, God, it seems, must curb his freedom of will at the danger line. When Israel's backsliding would drive them into exile, the Lord vowed:[13] *"And yet for all that, when they are in the land of their enemies, I will not reject them, neither will I abhor them, to destroy them utterly and to break my covenant with them; for I am the Lord their God."* God does not interfere with Israel's freedom of will, much as He endeavors to influence it in the direction of right and mercy. He but saves them, by His mercy, from the ultimate consequences of their misdeeds. But that is only because of the merits of their fathers, or because of the indestructible core of their goodness behind all their evil conduct. However, as for the nations which do not know the Lord, for the kings and potentates, who deliberately and maliciously oppose His standards and would ruin the world to possess it, if He were not to prevent the fulness of their fury, the work of His hands through the evil of one or some of His creatures would be laid waste, if not utterly destroyed. Thus the Lord, who created man free so that he might work out his salvation, must, as it were, limit his freedom, to save him and his neighbors from himself. In the creative moment, God did it seminally as He transmitted to man, when He gave him a soul, a deep desire to live on, in and through the family, in and through the community. But for the grace of God, however, manifest in any of these similar ways, human perversity might have obliterated His handi-work. That is how providence interferes with man's mad effort at self-destruction, from the first frenzy of Cain's through the bloody story of mass matricide, patricide, fratricide, to the terrifying glory of the Atomic Bomb.*

II. The Quest for Knowledge and the Resignation off the Goal

To know God, according to Maimonides, is a primary and the first commandment, the greatest duty of the Israelite, and of every human. While "we cannot penetrate to the essence of His nature,"[14] there are many ways to reach as clear and deep a knowledge of Him as our heart and mind can attain. Knowledge, certain and definite intuition, insight through a sharpened sense of harmony, through the awesome comprehension of His infinity, through the happy assurance of the cosmos in regular operation, through the feeling of communion with God in prayer, of His acceptance of earnest labor for one's soul or the common good, through the study of His Torah as a whole, and through devoted interest to the ideas underlying, or most likely to underlie, His laws: through all these experiences and endeavors, through the intuitive sympathy with His plan of life derived from full con-formity with His laws, one may gain a reconstructive vision of His mind, a glimpse of the unchanging on the fleeting screen of life.[15] What Plotinus had envisaged as man's sublimest level,[16] the cataclysmic identification of man with God in the ecstasy of seeing Him, that consummation can be brought about, as an abiding condition, through the disembodied unity of the finite with the infinite, the life and thought in Torah: a spiritual climate spelling the achievement of such penetrative and pre-vailing and normal communion, "even as the bride with her

---

* In a curious congruity, the skeptic and the saint may alike be vindicated. The love of right, and peace, even the stirring of sympathy and the passion for kindness, may perchance serve, together with these ideals, also the instinct for self-preservation. That may be why minorities are ever found to battle power-drunk majorities, or power-mad individuals. That may be the secret reason why, at times, the very murderous tyrant commits the fatal error which undoes his fell design. That is why other handicaps are found to arise, to limit his vision, to defeat his cunning plan, to lead him on to self-destruction.

groom," the beloved maiden with her beloved friend, intellect with sentiment, the soul athrob with the joy of receiving the spirit, the crown causing the emanation of the divine power[17] (as the mystic books variously phrase it). The knowledge of God thus means many things to many devotees of theosophic speculation, from the warm rationalism of Maimonides to the ordered ecstasy of Isaac Luria.

So that knowledge again is a goal, and the way, a promise, a challenge, and a harvest. *"Thou hast been made to see"*[18] the Lord's metaphysical image. Through knowledge thou hast scaled the wall of the garden. Through knowledge thou art granted a wide horizon, an infinite blueness of sky, and a foresight of threatening clouds. Through knowledge you see stumbling blocks and prepare to remove them. Through knowledge you see the way and the end, the *cul de sac* and the beckoning light. And yet man's knowledge is limited by the perception of his senses and the deductions his mind makes therefrom. With all the uncharted seas accessible to his bold mental vista, man becomes more and more conscious, with every advance, of the distance off the point of achievement, which seems to increase as it remains impervious to his frantic thrusts at truth beyond his level.

The Greeks were rational as well as ethical optimists. Aristotle taught:[19] "Use your mind, live in the road of the golden mean, and, granted a bit of good luck to push your intelligent boat in occasional muddy waters, you will achieve harmony, serenity, happiness." Saadya endorsed Socrates' rational optimism,[20] as, a thousand years later, the older Huxley sounded the triumphal tocsin of scientific assurance: "Just follow careful technique and all nature will yield its secrets, all doubts will vanish. Science will give you power, teach you order, ushering in the blessed millennium."

The twentieth century physicist and philosopher is less sanguine. He is equally wise and sad. To the sustained standards of modern clarity of view, the adolescent ebullience of the intellectual go-getter, sure of reaching his goal, seems as pointless as the whole-sale renunciation by the Alexandrinians of man-made salvation, and the vale-of-tears platform of "The Book of the Dead."

Yet another dilemma seems to loom large on our view: For the development of man's chance to fulfill his destiny, to gain intelligent and permanent control of the beasts, birds, plants, of life and all the riches of the earth, God granted man his mind and all its properties and faculties to use fruitfully. There may be many interpretations of the tree of knowledge of good and evil, but no matter what definition pleases us most, man,[21] *"lest he become like God,"* was cast out from the garden into the painful land without, painful not only for the thorns and thistles which at least might be cleared away, but for the ineluctable resignation: We must stop some distance off the goal. In all questing, post-laboratory and beyond logic, Einstein will agree, we ultimately reach but a world of symbols, i.e., arbitrary *as if*[22] terms and theorems. Whether knowledge or the acquisition thereof leads to inevitable physical decadence, as Jacob Klatzkin[23] has maintained, or to moral impotence in the twilight of the almost conquered empire of the absolute, God undeniably has done both: He granted us the entrance to the field *and* barred the way to the goal. Between the two, our tragedy and our glory are re-enacted in every age. The imperativeness of the grant is matched in significance only by the imperativeness, obvious since effected, of the limitation. We may now and then spasmodically grasp at new meaning, and all the time inch forward on an infinite road, but the dilemma will keep its challenge to the end of days.

III. Rewards and Punishments,
and the Safety Margin for an Ethical Personality

Of course God faces no dilemmas. It is only in our hard effort to read a consistent meaning into providence that such problems loom large in our consciousness. With Bahya we shall agree: a good deed is one which has been performed for the sake of the "good," not because of the ulterior motive of reward, whether this reward comes in the form of public approval, monetary compensation or social advancement. Aristotle[24] wins an ever new endorsement of his statement that a deed may be described as good only when it expresses, and springs from, a man's abiding good character. The deed may not be termed good even if it be benign in present motive, even if it has accidentally benefited someone. Conversely, a man might be evil though he committed no overt act socially hurtful or otherwise mean. The cause of his failure to commit an evil deed may be the fear of punishment. Murderous gangs are evil even when they are deterred from assault by an honest and swiftly moving police force or by courts of justice that cannot be influenced by political or other bribery.

In general, the assumption is morally right and borne out in the life of man that God rewards a good deed and punishes an evil one. That conviction is fundamental to all religion, and in its special framework is accepted as right and proper in all cognate ethical discussion. Yet here this dilemma presents itself to our thinking about God: When the rabbis suggest that no definite reward for a good deed is granted in this life, they anticipate the problem which Maimonides[25] elaborated. The suggestion there advanced embraces many facets of the matter.[26] He avers that there are small or large consequences of our acts that men prize as rewards. But he indicates that what may be received as an accessory interim reward represents only the pedagogical encouragement of the immature. In his intellectual and moral advance man will recognize that the ultimate reward of a good deed comes from the consciousness of the good performed and the effect on our character of our righteous or merciful conduct; just as the ultimate benefit from the study of the good book lies not, indeed, in degrees granted by the academy or in popular acclaim, but in the broadening and deepening of one's personality, which devoted preoccupation with the Torah bestows upon the student. In one form or another, then, rewards may be expected for good deeds performed, and penalties for evil committed. Yet if *every* good were rewarded, and *every* evil deed were punished, the development of an ethical personality would be almost impossible. Back of our readiness to perform such good deed would be the expectancy of ultimate reward, sooner or later, and every good deed would be no more than a long-time investment whose profit or dividend might be definitely counted upon. Similarly, many a man would successfully resist temptation to do evil because of his abject fear of inevitable punishment overtaking him, while very possibly remaining completely evil in his character, and awaiting only the opportunity to escape such punishment for the perpetration of the most gruesome atrocities. A modern example of this dark potentiality of the human mind is the Hitler regime, during which unimaginable horrors were deliberately planned and executed with fiendish accuracy and scientific deviltry by the Nazis, who felt sure that because of their well-nigh perfect crime of preparing the second world war, through "invincible superiority in arms and techniques," they could escape for a thousand years the penalty of their black regime*. Thus there remains but one way out: God, as it were, for a safety margin for the ethical nobility of human beings, "must" leave some good deeds unrewarded and some evil deeds unpunished. With reward thus not absolutely certain, it is feasible that man might do good for the sake of the good, and with punishment not absolutely inevitable, it might be feasible that man would shun evil because it is evil and not because he feared the judge's wrath or society's condemnation.

This does not, indeed, answer the questions resulting from earthquakes, the suffering of the obviously righteous, the death of an innocent child, and the tragic affliction of its parents. These problems seem to defy adequate answers, for "to know the mind of God" in each human catastrophe would mean "to be God-like," and we are never unaware of the limitations of our own intellect. His mercy, the high points of individual lives, as in the undisturbed cosmic order, will continue to offer potent arguments and dull the edge of private pain and public consternation in the mystery of suffering. But into the sphere of the particular problem apparent to our quest, light seems to enter from the door our meditations may have opened.

* * *

Added to these dilemmas might be that of every religious person. The Torah states:[27] *"Go after the Lord, your God, and*

---

* Recall the classic attitude of the Epicureans and their answers to queries probing their moral nihilism: Since they deny the essential relevancy of "good" and "evil," and we are restrained from e.g. murder only by fear of punishment, assurance of safety from prosecution would cause them to commit such acts.

cling to Him." The rabbis ask:[28] How can human beings go in
the way of God and cling to Him, Who is a spirit? They answer:
"Go in His ways, i.e., imitate His ethical qualities. As He is
merciful, be thou merciful; as He is gracious, be thou gracious."
So love of God implies a genuine desire to develop one's personality in the direction of His standards, and in approximation of
His pure being. Yet every sensible human being knows that we
can never reach His level, neither in our thinking nor in our
living. Thus, again we are constrained to move perpetually between the poles of our limitations and His perfection. The
essence of our position involves this dualism. The function alike
of faith and wisdom, implies our acceptance of both poles and of
the tension they always generate. We must not stay where we are,
in a Hobbesian state of nature. Yet we are constitutionally unable
to reach the goal: God-likeness. Between the two, lie the glory
and tragedy of man.

NOTES

1. Emun. II
2. *Moreh* III, 15
3. *Or Adonai*, II, 3
4. Isa. LV, 8
5. Talmud Babli Ber. 31b
6. Deut. XI, 26
7. T. B. Qidd. 40 a
8. Gen. XV, 6
9. Ibid. XIV, 23
10. Joseph Butler: "Upon Human Nature," II, III
11. Immanuel Kant: "Metaphysics of Morality" II
12. "Beyond Conscience," Introduction
13. *Lev.* XXVI, 44
14. *Yesode ha-Torah* I
15. Cf. commentary of R. Isaac Aramah on Exodus **XXXIII, 23**.
16. Enn. VI, 7
17. Midr. Shir Hashir. R., a, 1
18. Deut. IV, 35
19. Nich. Ethics, passim
20. Em.ve-Deoth, Introduction.
21. *Gen.* III, 5
22. Vaihinger's *Als Ob*
23. In *"Der Erkenntnistrieb als Lebens— und Todesprinzip"*
24. N.E. 2
25. In the introduction to his commentary on the tenth chapter of the Mishnah of
    Sanhedrin. See Qidd. 39b
26. Theodor Gompertz, Greek Thinkers, II, 2
27. Deut. XIII, 4
28. Ber. 33b

RABBINIC BACKGROUND OF THE FIVE DAILY PRAYERS IN ISLAM

BY DR. ABRAHAM I. KATSH

Rabbinic Background of the Five Daily Prayers In Islām

BY DR. ABRAHAM I. KATSH

IT IS INCUMBENT on every Moslem to pray five times daily[1] (at sunrise, mid-day, mid-afternoon, sunset, and before retiring) .[2] Goldziher in his article on Islām in the Jewish Encyclopedia regards the five daily prayers as of Persian influence.[3] Rabbi Simon Duran declares that Muḥammad borrowed the custom from the Jewish Day of Atonement.[4] Professor Torrey maintains that, in their anxiety to surpass the Jews in devotion, the followers of Muḥammad adopted the five daily prayers after his death, for "there is in the Koran no prescription of the *five* daily prayers, and it is not clear that they were instituted by Mohammed. It is not like him to ordain a five-fold service even for *one* day in the week. What he commands in the Koran is characteristic. It is simple, reasonable, and like other features of the new legislation in its adoption of an already existing ritual to Arabian conditions. The traditional Jewish prescription was three daily prayers, as e.g. in Dan. 6:11. In four passages (11:116, 17:80f., 50:38f., 76: 25f.) , all from the Mekka period, the prophet directs his followers to pray three times in the day: in the morning at eventide, *and in the night*—a time better suited to the Bedouin traveling under the stars than to the city-dweller."[5]

In addition to the four passages cited by Torrey, we find several other passages in the Koran which give indications of the practice of five daily prayers. Thus in 20:130 we read: "Bear patiently then what they say, and celebrate the praises[6] of thy Lord before the rising of the sun, and before its setting, and at times in the night celebrate them; and at the ends of the day, haply thou mayest please (Him) ." Here Muḥammad directs his followers to pray

at sunrise, sunset, and "at the ends of the day" i.e. before retiring.[7] In Sura 11 verse 116 Muhammad also directs his followers,
"And be thou steadfast in prayer at the two ends of the day, and
the (former and latter) parts of the night." Pickthall[8] renders
the last phrase "and in some watches of the night," whereas Ali[9]
translates it "in the first hours of the night". This would add,
immediately after sunset, an additional prayer to the prayers
mentioned in 17:80, i.e. "from the declining of the sun until the
dusk of the night, and the reading of the dawn." In 24:57 the
Koran also talks about "the prayer of dawn, and when ye put off
your clothes at noon, and after the evening prayer." Thus, the
sunrise prayer, the mid-day prayer, and the prayer before retiring are referred to in 17:80, the mid-afternoon prayer in 20:30,
and the sunset prayer in 11:116. According to Islāmic tradition,
it was the Prophet who told his followers that "Allah has made
obligatory the five prayers in every day and night."[10]

The rules and regulations concerning prayer in general in Islām,
would indicate that the five daily prayers have their background
in Jewish practices. Thus a Moslem, like a Jew, is encouraged to
pray often and as frequently as possible.[11] Prayers may be combined
or curtailed when one is on a journey or in time of danger. And
if recital of a prayer is forgotten, it may be uttered when re-
membered.[12] Prayers, too, must not be said in a loud voice nor
in a whisper. [13] Nor may a drunken man pray.[14] Similarly, the rules
pertaining to prayers for the community, for rain and others, are
all traceable to Jewish practices.[15] Some authorities even claim
that at the beginning of Islām, Moslems used to put on a *Tallit*
(prayer shawl) at services in the mosque.[16] It seems logical that
since most of the rituals were derived in the main from Jewish
usage,[17] that the five daily prayers should have originated from
the same source. Recent talmudic studies suggest that this is so.

Though the Bible is replete with prayers of all types, we find
no reference in biblical books, with the exception of Daniel,
which is of post-exilic origin, to prayer as a regular daily institution. In biblical times prayers were a personal matter. Many terms
such as berakah (from the Hebrew barok, to kneel), and tefillah
(from the Hebrew palel, to address a judge or high power),

shebah (adoration), and hallel (praise), are frequently used in the Bible, which would indicate that prayer was prevalent in Israel even in early times.

The beginning of the institution of prayers is to be traced to the time of the Babylonian exile. During that period many previously existing forms of public worship, such as the Temple and public sacrifices, were eliminated and a desire on the part of the individual Jew to commune with God resulted in prayer becoming a daily affair. Thus we read that Daniel's windows being open in his chamber towards Jerusalem, "he kneeled upon his knees three times a day and prayed and gave thanks before his God as he did aforetime."[18] We may rightly infer from this the custom of three daily services, morning (Shaharit),[19] afternoon (Minhah),[20] and evening (Maárib).[21]

According to the Talmud, the Great Assembly established the institution of daily prayers.[22] Important portions of the morning prayer were recited in the Temple,[23] which would indicate that regular daily services were in existence during the larger part of the Second Commonwealth. From the time of the destruction of the Temple, the Shemoneh 'Esreh (eighteen benedictions), also known as the 'Amidah, became an important part of the three daily services, though the recitation of some of the benedictions must have been in vogue much earlier. It was Rabbi Gamliel of the Academy of Jabneh,[24] who enacted that each worshipper should recite the Shemoneh 'Esreh. In order not to deviate from the original public recitation, he ruled that the Reader also repeat it in public. In the prayer book, the Shemá and the 'Amidah constitute the most important parts of the service, while the other parts are mainly supplementary. The Shemá as known is composed of verses of the following passages of the Pentateuch: Deuteronomy 6:4-9, dealing with the unity and love of God and observance of the precepts; Deuteronomy 11:13-21, emphasizing reward for the fulfillment of the laws and punishment for their transgression and the duty of teaching the Torah to the children; Numbers 15:37-41, enacting the law concerning the observance of the Zizit (fringes on the garment) and an exhortation to submit to the laws of God in remembrance of the Exodus.

The *Shemoneh 'Esreh* is divided into three parts. The first three prayers deal with praise of the Lord; the twelve middle ones with petitions; and the last three with extending thanks to the Lord. The morning and evening prayers contain, between the *Shemá* and the *Shemoneh 'Esreh*, a prayer for redemption known as *Ge'ullah*.

In the Talmud Babli,[25] there is controversy between Rabbi Johanan and Rabbi Joshua ben Levi, whether the prayer of *redemption* should be attached to the *Shemoneh 'Esreh* at the evening prayer or not. Rabbi Johanan holds that the prayer should be linked with it, while Rabbi Joshua maintains that it should not.[26] Without this connection there would be two separate prayers, the *Shema* and the *Shemoneh 'Esreh*. Otherwise there would be only one. The majority opinion agrees with Rabbi Johanan that the prayer for *redemption* should be attached (to the *'Amidah*) in the evening prayer. As for Shaharit, the morning prayer, all agree that the prayer of redemption *is* attached to the *Shemoneh 'Esreh*. Therefore, according to the Babylonian Talmud, we have three daily prayers.

Professor Louis Ginzberg in his monumental study on Talmud Yerushalmi,[27] maintains that the institution of prayer originally constituted *five* daily prayers, instead of the known three. Ginzberg postulates that according to the Yerushalmi *all* scholars agree that the Jews in Arabia did not attach the prayer of Redemption to the Shemoneh 'Esreh in the evening prayer.[28] Thus the Shemá and the *Shemoneh 'Esreh* were *two* separate prayers. In early times, the custom was to recite the Shemá at home, before retiring and immediately upon rising. Before the institution of prayer, the people uttered the *Shemá* in the morning at dawn and *before* the rising of the sun; i.e. between rising and the hours of work. This practice was based on the biblical verse, "and when thou liest down and when thou risest up."[92] Later, when prayers became an institution, the morning prayer was recited in the Synagogue after the rising of the sun. The Shemá too was recited in the Synagogue at the usual time. The hardship of congregating twice, once for the *Shemá* and once for the "prayer" (Shemoneh 'Esreh) was facilitated by reciting the *Shemá* closer to sunrise, followed immediately by the "prayer." Though there were still many who continued to recite the *Shemá* at home and joined the congregation for prayer later on, the general practice was to combine the two. This finally led to the assumption that it was obligatory to attach the prayer of *redemption* to the *Shemoneh 'Esreh*.

Thus, we learn that the Jews in Arabia during the talmudic period, really met five times daily for prayer in the synagogue; twice for the recitation of the *Shemá*,[30] and three times for the three regular prayers.[31] For practical reasons, the two prayers in the morning[32] were combined into one, as were the two prayers in the evening.[33] The five daily prayers may thus have been instituted by Muḥammad as a result of the early Jewish practice of meeting five times daily for prayer.[34]

FOOTNOTES

1. *Fajr* (morning); *Zuhr* (early afternoon); *'Aṣr* (late afternoon); *Maghrib* (sunset); *'Isha'* (night).

2. Islam considers the institution of prayer as part of the Sunna. See ‏א. נ. פולק,‏
‏דברי ימי הערבים, ירושלים, תש"ו, ע' קלב.‏

3. p. 653

4. Simon Duran ‏קשת ומגן‏ in ‏אוצר טוב‏ (ed Steinschneider), Berlin, 1881, p. 14
‏„ולפי שידע שהיותר נכבד שביתי ישראל לתפלה ולתשובה הוא יום הכפורים ויש‏
‏בו חמש תפלות תקן להם חמש תפלות בכל יום.‏
However, it is questionable whether *Musaf* is a separate prayer and not an extension of the Shaḥarit. cf. ‏רמבם, הלכות תפלה, פ"א, הה" וח"ו.‏
Rabbi Duran also maintains that Ramaḍān is of Jewish influence (*ibid.* p. 14)
‏ולפי שהוא (יוה"כ) צום ותשובה תקן להם שלשים צומות (יום)."‏
See also E. Mittwoch, *Zur Entstehungsgeschichte des islanischen Gebets und Kultus*, Berlin, 1913, pp. 36ff.

5. Ch. C. Torrey, *The Jewish Foundation of Islam*, New York, 1933, p.

6. "Celebrate the praises" refers to prayers, as shown by the context in 20:132: "Bid thy people prayer, and persevere in it." Cf. Ps. 68:20; Ps. 78:4; Ps. 96:3; 105:2.

7. Here the two evening prayers are spoken of together, while the sunrise prayer and mid-afternoon prayer are indicated.

8. M. M. Pickthall, *The Meaning of the Glorious Koran*, London, 1930, p. 234.

9. M. M. Ali, *The Holy Qur-ān*, Lahore, 1935, p. 474

10. Al-Bukhārī, *Recueil des Traditions Mohamétanes* (Krehl ed.) Leyde, 1862-1908. Vol. I. p. 354.

11. ‏שכל המרבה בתפלה נענה (תלמוד ירושלמי, ברכות, פ"ד, ה"א)‏; *Yalkut Shim'oni,* Vol. II, §847; Bu. Vol. I, p. 181

12. 4:10; Bu. Vol. I, p. 157

13. 17:111; cf. 1 Sam. 1:13; Berakot 31b.

14. 4:46; cf. Berakot 31b.

15. J. W. Hirschberg ‏קצ"ז, ע' תש"ו, תל אביב, בערב היהודים.‏

16. Hirschberg, *ibid.* p. 197

17. Cf. A. J. Wensinck, "Die Entstehung der Muslimischen Reinheitsgesetzegebung;" in *Der Islam*, V (1914), pp 62 ff.

18. **Daniel 6:11**

19. שחרית.

20. מנחה.

21. מעריב; cf. Talmud Yeushalmi, Ber. 1 and *Numbers Rabbah* 2, 1.

22. Berakot 33a; Megilot 17 b. See also Solomon Zeithn "An historical study of the first Canonization of the Hebrew Liturgy," JQR N, S. XXVI (1946), pp. 211 f. XXXVIII (1948), pp. 289 f.;

23. משנה תמיד, ה, ע"א.

24. c. 90 B.C.E.

25. ברכות, ד, ע"ב.

26. *Ibid.*; cf. ג. ד, תענית משנה ; א, ה, תמיד משנה.

27. **Louis Ginzberg**, *A Commentary on the Palestinian Talmud*, New York, 1941, Vol. I, pp. 68-75.

28. *Ibid.* Vol. I, p. 68

29. Deut. 6:7; 11:9

30. Ginzberg, *op. cit*, p. 64

31. i.e. *Shemoneh 'Esreh*. Verses 79-81 in Sura 26 recall the prayers in the Eighteen Benedictions.

32. i.e. the *Shemā* and the *Shemoneh 'Esreh*. Moslem tradition, too, provides that what the days are short, the *Zuhr* and the *'Asr prayers* may be combined.

33. **Ginzberg, *op. cit.* p. 63.**

34. *Ibid.* pp. 74-75. For a fuller discussion see the author's book *Judaism in Islām*, New York, 1954, pp. 3-13.

DYSPEPSIA—CAUSES AND NATURE

BY ELIHU KATZ, M.D.

Dyspepsia—Causes and Nature

BY ELIHU KATZ, M.D.

I AM GRATEFUL to the members of the Jewish Academy of Arts and Sciences for the kind invitation to address you this evening.

Gastro-enterology is one of the most important specialties of internal medicine. When one considers, however, the frequency of digestive disturbances and the fact that a great many diseases are initiated by digestive symptoms, the importance of this specialty is evident. Gastro-enterology, as a specialty, covers a wide field and it is, therefore, impossible within the scope of this paper to discuss all phases of digestion. I have limited the subject to a discussion of dyspepsia, its nature and causes. Dyspepsia is a commonly used term and suggests a disturbance in the digestion of food, either in the stomach or the intestines. Each part of the digestive tract, from the mouth to the lower end of the large intestines, has its own particular work to do. Each part forms and secretes its own juices which help in digestion of food. There are many organs connected with the gastro-intestinal tract whose particular function is to assist the digestive process. They are known as accessory organs of digestion. The chief ones are the salivary glands, the liver with its gall bladder and biliary ducts, and the pancreas.

The purpose of digestion is to prepare food for its entrance into the blood. This preparation is necessary to make the food suitable for use by the body for growth and development, maintenance and repair of tissue, production of heat and energy, protection against diseases, and other essential functions. Digestion is said to be perfect when the stomach and intestines function well. When, for any reason, the stomach or intestines have become disturbed, there is an interference with their work. This means that digestion is no longer perfect. Symptoms are thus produced, and grouped under the general term dyspepsia.

In explaining dyspepsia, it is necessary to consider briefly the main facts of digestion. This will show how readily digestion may become disturbed by an interference with the digestive organs. Digestion begins in the mouth with mastication. During mastication, the salivary glands secrete a watery digestive juice or saliva. Saliva contains the important enzyme or ferment known as ptyalin which converts the starches into maltose or sugar. Proper chewing of food is important for digestion. If food is gulped, more work is thrown upon the stomach. Gulping or bolting of food frequently leads to dyspepsia. Fast eating leads to swallowing large amounts of air. This causes the stomach to become distended, resulting in discomfort and a desire to belch gas. In the effort to bring up this gas, more air is swallowed, resulting in more distention and more discomfort.

From the mouth the food passes into the stomach, where it mixes with the stomach juices. The stomach pours out this juice within five minutes after food enters, and may continue to do so for several hours.

One of the chief characteristics of the normal stomach is its ability to handle all varieties of foods. Any change in this ability may be the first indication of a stomach disturbance.

In the small intestines, the combined juices of the small bowel itself, the liver, and pancreas take part in the further digestion of the food. The proteins and fats are digested and the digestion of the starches is also completed. From the small intestines most of the products of digestion passes into the blood and lymphatics. It takes three to four hours for digestion to be completed in the small intestines and about 94% of the available food is absorbed. What is not taken up by the blood and lymphatics passes into the large intestines or colon by the combined contractions of the muscles of the small intestines. Virtually no digestion occurs in the colon and absorption plays no important part. What remains of the ingested material has now become waste. As the waste is forced through the large intestines by the contractions of its muscles, some of the fluid is taken up and the waste becomes more and more solid. When this is finally passed out, digestion is complete.

It is clear that changes in the secretions or interference with the contractions may easily disturb digestion. The importance of keeping the stomach and intestines in perfect condition is also evident. Digestion takes place without any distress or pain, and a person in good health is never aware of what goes on during digestion; this then means that a disturbance in digestion has occurred. Such disturbances may arise from diseases, as ulcers or cancer. In these abnormal conditions, actual structural changes in the tissues of the gastro-intestinal tract are present. The damage may be slight or very extensive.

Important, also, is the fact that functional disturbances may not alone arise from secretory or motor causes within the tract itself but may be induced by abnormal conditions of other organs.

The organs of the body are so related that an irritation in one will set up a disturbance in another. Dyspepsia is a very frequent occurrence in gall bladder disease.

Many patients who believe that they have dyspepsia, because of stomach trouble, are on the contrary really affected with a gall bladder condition. A similar relationship exists between the appendix and the stomach. Appendicitis is frequently the cause of dyspepsia for which the stomach or the intestine is wrongly held responsible.

Of all dyspepsias, functional dyspepsia is most common. It occurs in people who are otherwise well. It is most frequent between the ages of 18 and 45, and affects women more often than men. Among the many possible causes for functional dyspepsia, the following may be mentioned:

1. Eating too often and too much.

2. Eating when exhausted or forcing food when not hungry.

3. Improper chewing and rapid eating.

4. Eating of foods that are indigestible and foods too hot or cold.

5. Diet poor in minerals, vitamins, or other necessary substances.

6. Constant use of highly seasoned and fried foods.

7. Use of too many liquids while eating, either coffee, tea, or water.

8. Irregularity of meals.

9. Excessive use of alcohol and tobacco.

10. Overwork.

11. Worry, anxiety, and other emotional disturbances.

Gall bladder is the chief instigator. Abnormal conditions of the gall bladder are the most frequent cause of digestive symptoms. These symptoms may simulate dyspepsia of peptic ulcer. Indeed, differential diagnosis may be most difficult. Abdominal discomfort with a feeling of pain, gaseous eructation, nausea, and vomiting commonly occur.

The next in frequency is the disease known as peptic ulcer. An ulcer may be described as a crater-like break in the continuity of the external or internal surface of the body, forming an open sore. They occur in the stomach, lower end of the esophagus, and the duodenum. Ulcers may be acute or chronic. They are fairly common, for statistically it has been estimated that one out of every ten at some time or other during life has suffered with an peptic ulcer. Males and females are affected about equally by gastric ulcer, but duodenal ulcers are more frequent in the male. They occur mostly between the ages of 30 to 50 years. Many factors are involved, two important ones being the hereditary tendency to ulcer formation in certain individuals and the increased acidity of the stomach. The most common digestive symptoms of peptic ulcers are pain, gaseous eructations, water brash, heartburn, nausea, vomiting, constipation, loss of weight, and bleeding.

Another most frequent dyspepsia is due to the appendix. Here, there is pain in the lower right side. Occasionally, the pain is referred to the region of the stomach and is associated with heartburn, belching, gas, and nausea after meals. Digestive symptoms are most apt to follow the taking of a laxative which irritates the inflamed appendix.

Cancer is the most dreaded of all diseases. However, it is not invariably fatal if diagnosed in time. If discovered in the early stages it can be eradicated. If diagnosed even late the patient still has an excellent chance of recovery. This is the best possible argument for the complete investigation of patients suffering with indigestion.

The earliest symptoms are loss of appetite or even distaste for certain foods, with a sense of fullness or nausea after meals. These are especially significant if they occur in persons over 35 years of age who have never had any previous attacks of indigestion. These should be considered to have cancer of the stomach until proven otherwise. Later on, pain is present. This gradually becomes more severe and is less relieved by alkaline foods or vomiting.

In all types of dyspepsia it is observed that symptoms are usually the same, but may vary in intensity. Unfortunately, there is no constant relationship between symptoms and cause, functional or organic. Therefore it is impossible to list a set of digestive symptoms of a dyspepsia as characteristic or specific for any cause. An additional complication is the fact that patients vary in their interpretation of digestive sensations, and many symptoms described may be misleading and turn the doctor from the real cause. In other words, the gastro-intestinal tract is a tract of mystery.

The following are most frequent symptoms noted in most dyspepsias:

1. Mild discomfort to pain in the pit of the stomach, which may or may not be related to eating.

2. Loss of appetite.

3. Difficulty in swallowing.

4. Bloating, fullness, or tightening immediately or soon after eating.

5. Belching.

6. Regurgitation—portions of food or fluid coming back into the mouth and expectorated. The regurgitation of a sour fluid is "water brash."

7. Heartburn—the regurgitation of the partly digested food from the stomach into the gullet with a burning sensation.

8. Nausea and vomiting. Nausea may occur without vomiting and vomiting without nausea.

9. Constipation—the single symptom mostly complained of and so typical of dyspepsia.

Dyspepsia, furthermore, may include such general symptoms as drowsiness, listlessness, dizziness, headaches, palpitation of the heart, irritability, nervousness, fatigue, and weakness. When the symptoms are definitely related to the stomach, they are referred to as "indigestion."

In this presentation, the purpose has been to clarify, in a general way, dyspepsia, its possible causes and symptoms, and to stress, more particularly, the importance of diagnosis. A correct diagnosis with proper treatment will bring prompt relief and may prevent serious complication. Frequently many patients rightfully wish to know the explanation of their symptoms, and they ply their physician with queries, why pain, nausea, and constipation, and so on. With a better understanding of the nature of this digestive disorder, the patient usually gives better cooperation. This is one of the most essential factors in successful treatment of dyspepsia.

THE INFLUENCE OF MAIMONIDES ON SCHOLASTIC THOUGHT

BY REV. DR. LEE J. LEVINGER

The Influence of Maimonides
on Scholastic Thought

BY REV. DR. LEE J. LEVINGER

MAIMONIDES came at the end of an epoch in the Jewish and Moslem worlds, but at the beginning of one for Christian scholasticism. Islam, after the death of Averroes, his contemporary, had no philosopher left and desired none. The Moslem world was for the moment in a mood of bitter reaction and of suppression of all independent thought. Judaism likewise was at the end of an era of constructive and fruitful philosophy—though not for the same reason. Persecution to Jewry came from without rather than from within, and the age of persecution ushered in during the life of Moses ben Maimon only spread more widely and bore more heavily during the centuries to follow. The attempt to master the world by the weapons of the intellect had come as always during an age of toleration, when the mind was free to soar. The age of repression which followed became for the leading minds of Jewry an age of flight from reality, instead. It was the day of Kabbalah as the only variation from concentration on the law. The sole exception came in the occasional aspiring Talmud student who, in his own person, burst forth to the world of pure thought. Such a man was Spinoza, such another was Mendelssohn, and in both of them the influence of Maimonides was potent. A third, Solomon Maimon, proudly proclaimed that connection by assuming the name of his ideal philosopher.

But Christian thought in that thirteenth century had just emerged from the period of dialectic and epistemology to grasp the great problems of science and metaphysics. That was the century of the universal philosophers, the writers of Summae which included in a single system every phase of thought, from physics to theology. The prime fructifying influence on the thought of these men was the great rationalistic system of Aristotle, which they were just receiving in Latin translations. They had these epoch-making works in their hands for the first time, as well as the more mystical systems of Plato and the neo-Platonists. Their central problem, then, was how to be at once Aristotelians and Christians; to include in a single system the science and rational philosophy of the Greeks and the religion which they had inherited and developed through the Church.

But it happened that two other groups of thinkers had already grappled with this same problem in only slightly different form. Both Moslems and Jews had made the same attempt, and their problems of God, of psychology, of ethics, of matter and form, were on exactly the same plane as those of the Christians. The scholastic thinkers, then, received two well thought out interpretations of Aristotle to aid them in their task. The one was the Commentary on Aristotle by Averroes, the Moslem judge of Cordova; the other, the "Guide to the Perplexed" of Maimonides. Averroes, on rapid inspection, proved heretical; his doctrine of the World Soul led to a denial of personality and of immortality; his theory of matter and form implied, if it did not definitely teach, pantheism. The Averroist heresy became a significant bypath in scholasticism. But in Maimonides the Christian thinkers found a religious philosophy in harmony with their own position and filling many of their own needs. It was based on Aristotle, indeed, and showed the same robust mastery of the materials of thought which distinguished that philosopher. It reinterpreted Jewish faith in terms of the modern science of the twelfth century. But it did not desert the fundamentals of religion; instead, it broke away from Aristotle at precisely those points where he came directly into conflict with revelation. Hence it was Maimonides rather than Averroes who interpreted Aristotle for the Christian world. A Latin version of the Guide was ready for them, made early in the thirteenth century from the Hebrew version of Judah Harizi.

The proper consideration of this subject in detail would

demand at least as much space as the two volumes which Jacob Gutmann has devoted to the relation of the scholastics to Jewish philosophy in general, for the chief of their relationships was that with Maimonides; Gabirol came second; and other Jewish thinkers appear in their works only as random references. Here we can only give the headings, which may be filled in at leisure by the student.

William of Auvergne, who was chiefly an admirer of Gabirol, knew the Guide and quoted it copiously, though not by name, with regard to scientific questions. Alexander of Hales, founder of the Franciscan school of thought, owed far more to Maimonides, in both science and theology, although he mentions the name of Rabbi Moyses only three times. Other Franciscans, such as Bonaventura and Duns Scotus, rely on Maimonides' interpretations in many instances; in fact, Duns follows him in the crucial problem of relation of faith and reason.

But the most profound result of Maimonides' work came through that school which was most hospitable to the rational thought of Aristotle, the Dominicans. Here his influence was paramount; these men, who were themselves sober, rationalistic thinkers, could not accept the heretical interpretation of Averroes and needed the aid of one who before them had approached the same problems from the standpoint of faith, of revealed religion. The influence of Maimonides on Albert the Great and Thomas Aquinas, then, ran through many parts of their system of thought, and was decisive in several crucial issues. Albert in particular quotes Maimonides hundreds of times under the name, Rabbi Moses the Egyptian. He does not rely on him in strictly scientific or logical problems, but rather in the field which Maimonides specially covered in the Guide, the relation between faith and reason and the interpretation of Scripture. He needed guidance in this critical point of the relation of Aristotle to revealed religion.

We may trace this influence at a number of points. Both Albert and Thomas use Maimonides' proofs for the existence of God, and Thomas follows him alone, going so far as to reject the *a priori* proof of St. Anselm. These proofs are all *a posteriori,* and derive indirectly from Aristotle, being based on the nature of the world and particularly on motion. Both Christians accept his treatment of the attributes of God, especially his idea that the attributes are identical with the divine nature, and that God can best be defined negatively. Both follow Maimonides and depart from Aristotle in the crucial question of the eternity of matter versus its creation; in accepting creatio ex nihilo they, like their Jewish predecessor, definitely choose a religious philosophy over a materialistic one. They followed him in part in his theory of angels and very largely in his psychological interpretation of Scripture, which had so shocked many of his Jewish opponents. They used many of his ethical concepts, particularly his definitions of sin and punishment. Most important of all, they leaned greatly on the theory of the relation of faith to reason. Here Thomas, like Maimonides, felt that the two must be in complete harmony, for both were the voice of God to man; still, revelation makes clear to mankind many truths which might be reached by the intellect with difficulty, if at all. The central character of these problems in a religious philosophy indicates the vital role which the system of Maimonides played in the thought of the two great Dominicans, whose system became dominant in the later Middle Ages and is still the official Catholic philosophy.

Through Thomas Aquinas, with his tremendous influence on all thought up to Kant, Maimonides became a part of the main stream of world philosophy. Both as a transmitter and as an original thinker, he was an important link in the chain that led from Aristotle to Thomas and from Thomas to Descartes. Through Thomas he influenced Descartes and the moderns. Spinoza was influenced by him in two ways, through Thomas also directly; Leon Roth has pointed out that entire passages in the Tractatus Theologico-Politicus were copied directly from the Guide. Roth even works out, in a brilliant essay in the "Legacy of Israel," a connection of Maimonides with Kant, which I must quote in part. "To link Kant with Maimonides is not so absurd as appears at first sight. The scholastic synthesis lived on till Kant, some would say after Kant, too; and in the making of that system

Maimonides, through the Latin version of the Guide, took a direct and leading part. It is not then a matter for surprise that the material and arrangement of the 'transcendental dialectic' should reflect the structure of the Guide; the Kantian 'ideal of reason,' the Maimonidean God of whom even the attribute of existence is predicted only *per analogiam*; the 'critical' inquiry itself, the discussion by Maimonides of the nature and instruments of knowledge."

Perhaps the direct indebtedness of Kant to Maimonides is not so great as Dr. Roth suggests; the indirect legacy from him, through Thomas, to all western thought, is certainly an enormous one. As a factor in the development of philosophy at a critical juncture, Maimonides has left a deep impress on later ages. His mastery of Greek science and metaphysics, his reconciliation of them with revealed religion, his attempt to construct a unified system which should be at once a religious philosophy and a reasonable religion, and subject to this aim, his mastery of Jewish law, Scriptural study, and the entire body of twelfth century science—these made the work of Maimonides worthy of study by those who followed him. And the acceptance of so many of his ideas in their systems have resulted in an enduring influence of wide scope and deep significance.

Bibliography

Some material on this subject appears in lives of Maimonides, such as those of Yellin and Abrahams, Hünz, and Zeitlin.

Specialized treatments appear in:

Legacy of Israel: art. by Charles Singer and Leon Roth.

Roth: Spinoza, Descartes, and Maimonides.

Guttman, J.: Die Scholastik des 13n Jahrhunderts in ihren Beziehungen zum Judenthum und zur Jüdischen Literatur.

David Neumark: Geschichte der Jüdischen Philosophie des Mittelalters, vol. 1, book 1, chapter 3.

MOSES MAIMONIDES
PHYSICIAN AND SCIENTIST

BY DAVID I. MACHT, M. D., F.A.C.P., PHAR. D., LITT. D.

Moses Maimonides
Physician and Scientist

BY DAVID I. MACHT, M. D., F. A. C. P., PHAR. D., LITT. D.

IT IS INTRINSICALLY true of science that it is ever going forward, changing and still advancing, always searching and researching for truth but only rarely reaching the absolute and fundamental. This very characteristic of science being always incomplete and ever looking forward to tomorrow is well expressed by the Hebrew term *da'ath,* which grammatically is the construct or incomplete form of *de'ah.* Many of the subjects which were discussed with so much fervor fifty years ago are almost forgotten now, and many an important discovery made today will probably be a platitude a year hence. For this reason, a complete estimate of the work of any scientist or medical man can only be made in relation to the age in which he lived, while a minute and detailed analysis of individual experimental and empirical data which he might have contributed is of interest chiefly to the specialist in any particular field of knowledge.

When studying the lives of great men in any field of endeavor, however, we usually discern certain trends of thought, philosophical attitudes, fundamental discoveries or methods of approach which we immediately recognize as new, original, and marking milestones in the development of a particular department of science, art, or other field of human endeavour and contributing significantly to the progress of civilization. Such fundamental contributions to the heritage of mankind are the earmarks of true genius and of genuine leaders in the arts, sciences, and humanities. Another interesting feature noted on studying the lives of such great men is the impressive fact that, whereas science is essentially transitory and ephemeral or, at most, annual in character, the general emotions and fervor that animated our scientific predecessors, their love of truth and appreciation of its value, the stimulus of scientific imagination, and the hope of achievement for the benefit of fellowman that inspired them—whether eighty or eight hundred years ago—remain relatively unchanged; and they are worthy of emulation and reiteration in these troubled times when even science and the art of healing are no longer looked upon as universal and cosmopolitan and are tainted and distorted by prejudice and hatred, be it of race, creed, or nationality.

Medicine is generally regarded as both a science and an art; and history tells us that Maimonides excelled in both of these. He was the leading scientist in medicine of his time and also the adept practitioner in the art of healing. His fame as physician or clinician is attested by the esteem of his contemporaries and posterity. Thus, the Arabic physician and historian, Osaibya, wrote of him that "He, Abu Amram Musa ben Maimuni, was a man deeply versed in the sciences and philosophy, who both in theoretical and practical medicine held the foremost place among the physicians of his time." The poet, Alsaid Ibn-Sina Almulk, wrote the following verses concerning him:

"Galen's art heals only the body,
  But Abu Amram's (Maimonides') the body and soul;
  With his wisdom he could heal the sickness of ignorance.
  If the moon would but submit to his art,
  He would deliver her of her spots at the time of full moon,
  Cure her of the periodic defects,
  And at the time of her conjunction save her from waning."

Furthermore, we know that by reason of his medical skill and erudition Maimonides became the special physician of Saladin, greatest of all the sultans. After the Crusade this renowned Jew was asked by Richard Coeur de Leon to desert his royal Saracen employer and go with him to England, which he declined to do. It is moreover interesting to learn that the illustrious prototype of the physician, Al Hakim, so vividly described by Sir Walter Scott in "The Talisman," is generally taken to have been Maimonides.

The duties of Maimonides as a physician were more strenuous than those of the modern practitioner and yet, like all great men, he found sufficient time with all his practice to devote to science, Hebrew lore, philosophy, and the humanities, and to function as Chief Rabbi or *Nagid*. Many of us are quite familiar with the famous letter he wrote to one of his disciples, Juda Ibn Tibbon, a letter which became a classic in Hebrew literature and without which no estimate of Rambam can be adequate.

"Now, God knows that in order to write this to you I have escaped to a secluded spot, where people would not think to find me, sometimes leaning for support against the wall, sometimes lying down on account of my excessive weakness, for I have grown old and feeble. With respect to your wish to come here to me, I cannot but say how greatly your visit would delight me, for I truly long to communicate with you and would anticipate our meeting with even greater joy than you. Yet I must advise you not to expose yourself to the perils of the voyage, for beyond seeing me and my doing all I could to honor you, you would not derive any advantage from your visit. Do not expect to be able to confer with me for even one hour either by day or by night; for the following is my daily occupation: I dwell in Mizr (Fostat) and the Sultan resides at Kahira; those two places are two Sabbath day's journeys (one and a half miles) distant from each other. My duties to the Sultan are very heavy. I am obliged to visit him every day, early in the morning; and when he, or any of his children, or any of the inmates of his harem are indisposed, I dare not quit Kahira but must stay during the greater part of the day in the palace. It also frequently happens that one or two of the officers fall sick and I must attend to their healing. Hence, as a rule, I repair to Kahira very early in the day and even if nothing unusual happens, I do not return to Mizr until the afternoon. Then I am almost dying with hunger. I find the antechambers filled with people, both Jews and gentiles, nobles and common people, judges and bailiffs, friends and foes—a mixed multitude who await the time of my return. I dismount from my animal, wash my hands, go forth to my patients, and entreat them to bear with me while I partake of some light refreshment, the only meal I take in twenty-four hours. Then I go forth to attend to my patients, write prescriptions and directions for their several ailments. Patients go in and out until nightfall, and sometimes even, I solemnly assure you, until two hours and more in the night. I converse with them, and prescribe for them while lying down from sheer fatigue; and when night falls I am so exhausted that I can scarcely speak. In consequence of this, no Israelite can have any private interview with me except on Sabbath Day. On that day the whole congregation, or at least the majority, come unto me after the morning service, when I instruct them as to their proceedings during the whole week; we stay together a little until noon, when they depart. Some of them return and read with me after the afternoon service until evening prayers. In this manner I spend that day. I have here related to you only a part of what you would see if you were to visit me."

Turning now to the contributions of Maimonides as a medical scientist, we find a long list of writings dealing with a great variety of scientific subjects, and particularly with experimental and empirical clinical medicine. Inasmuch as it is impossible for any scholar entirely to separate his varied interests from each other, a great deal of valuable medical material, particularly of a hygienic character, may be found in both the theological and philosophical works of Maimonides. Thus, his great Mishneh Torah, or Code of Jewish Law, contains most interesting advice on hygiene, which is surprisingly modern in tone. Similarly, Maimonides' famous philosophical treatise, "Guide to the Perplexed," contains scattered references to medicine and other sciences. The bulk of Maimonides' contributions, however, are contained in his purely scientific works (written for the most part in Arabic), which number at least twenty and may be conveniently classified under five headings.

I. Expositions and commentaries on older authorities:
1. *Pirque Mosheh* (aphorisms).
2. Commentary on Hippocrates.
3. Compend of Galen.
4. Translation of Avicenna.

II. Works of a hygienic character:
 1. *De Regimine Sanitatis.*
 2. Notes on dietetics, written for Saladin's son.
 3. The ethics of Maimonides, which deals not only with conduct but also with general care of the body.
 4. Works on social and sex hygiene.

III. Works of a physiological and pharmacological character:
 1. Treatise on foods.
 2. Treatise on materia medica.
 3. *Sefer Hassamim,* or "Toxicology."

IV. Works on special subjects:
 1. Hemorrhoids.
 2. Gout.
 3. Asthma.
 4. Mental diseases.
 5. Accidents and emergency treatment.

V. "Etiology and Pathology of Diseases."

The *Pirque Mosheh,* written between 1187 and 1190, is a collection of some fifteen hundred aphorisms (in twenty-five sections or chapters), taken largely from older writers, Hippocrates, Galen, Al-Razi, Avenzoar, and others, but full of critical notes and additions or corrections by Rambam. Written originally in Arabic, it was translated into Hebrew and later into Latin, and deals with every phase of medicine—anatomy, physiology, pathology, clinical symptomatology, materia medica, and therapeutics. Of the second group, the *Tadbir al-sihha* is a "Makrobiotik," or work on personal hygiene and dietetics, written about 1198 for *al-Malik al-Afdal,* Saladin's eldest son. Originally written in Arabic, it was translated and published in Hebrew in recent years in the periodical *Kerem Hemed* (III, 9-31).

Of the third group, the *Risālat al-fādilāyya* is perhaps the most important. In Hebrew, it is known as *Sefer Hassamim,* "Book of Poisons," or *Ha ma'amar Ha-nikbad.* This work on toxicology was written in 1199 and translated into various languages. The Latin translation, *De Venenis,* was used extensively by physicians in the fourteenth century. A German translation with notes by the late Dr. Steinschneider appeared in Virchow's Archiv (LVII). The sultan requested Maimonides to write this work on account of the numerous cases of poisoning, especially by poisonous animals, which were prevalent in his time. The work is extremely interesting to the modern pharmacologist and toxicologist because of the large amount of practical and useful information it contains. One section deals with bites of venomous insects and reptiles—scorpions, spiders, bees, wasps, and snakes. Another section discusses bites inflicted by quadrupeds and by men. Here there is a long discussion of bites by mad dogs. The great length of the incubation period in rabies is emphasized. The importance of ligation and suction in treatment of poison wounds is also stressed in this connection. "The first thing to do is to apply a tight band above the bitten part so as to prevent the poison gaining entrance to the body. While this is being done, an assistant should make incisions in and about the wound; and then, after rinsing one's mouth with oil, or with oil and wine, one should thoroughly suck the wound, being careful to spit out everything taken into the mouth. He who so sucks the wound should have no sore places in the mouth, nor any carious tooth. Should sucking be impossible, cupping may be resorted to." Another section deals with vegetable poisons such as opium, henbane, and other solanaceae, and toadstools. Still another describes such mineral poisons as verdigris, arsenic, and litharge.

Of the fourth group, the treatise on accidents, written about 1200, and known in Hebrew as *Teshubot 'al she'elot peratyyot* and in Latin, as *De Causis Accidentium,* is of special interest. It contains many prescriptions and formulae of other physicians, followed by some of his own, all of the latter being notable for their simplicity and medicinal value. In his work on asthma, *Maquāla-fi-l-rabw,* written about 1190, stress is laid on the importance of diet and climate for asthmatic patients. In the treatise on hemorrhoids, *Maquāla fí-l-bawāsir,* we find a discussion which compares well with the most modern tests on the subject. Indigestion and constipation are stressed as etiological factors; diet is considered as of paramount importance in the treatment; and surgical manipulations are discussed.

Finally, in his great work, *De Causis et Indiciis Morborum,* or "Etiology and Pathology of Diseases," there is a comprehensive treatise on the "Science and Practice of Medicine," to which I shall refer later. From this work, as well as from his *Sefer Hassamim* or Toxicology, we learn that Maimonides was centuries ahead of his time in his views on pharmacotherapy. He reveals a marked opposition to polypharmacy, or shotgun prescriptions (that is, complicated mixtures of obscure medicaments), and recommends only simple remedies and drugs which he had tested himself or the action of which had been established by recognized medical authorities. He was bitterly opposed to astrology and other occult arts in which the Arabs were so fond of dabbling. "The eyes look forward and not backward," he writes in one of his letters. The use of amulets and incantations in medical treatment he considered a sin and an abomination. A quack he called a murderer. "In minor ailments," he wrote, "nature cures the body without the need of medicinal remedies, if the patient only follows certain dietetic regulations. Where, however, the services of a physician are required, he should see to it that he aids nature in her beneficial course. Most of the doctors err in their treatment. In endeavoring to assist nature, they weaken the body with their prescriptions."

An examination of Maimonides' medical and scientific works reveals a number of important original conceptions with regard to medicine, in which he anticipated some of his colleagues by at least seven, if not eight, hundred years. In the first place, Maimonides, far in advance of his age, seems to have taken the modern attitude in regarding disease from the *etiological* or the causal standpoint, on the one hand, and to have stressed *pathological changes* produced by disease, on the other. It is regrettable that his most important work along this line, *De Causis et Indiciis Morborum,* has never been translated and is still lying in manuscript in the archives of Oxford and Paris. Concerning this work a famous medical writer, Alfred Nossig, has the following to say, "The very manner in which he undertakes his task in this his greatest work, the very fact that seven hundred years before the medicine of today, he already looks upon disease from the etiological point of view, his search for the *causes* of sickness—point to the man's keen intellect, and explain why he was regarded as such a great physician and rose to such fame."

In the second place, we find that Maimonides, in the most advanced spirit of the twentieth century, laid the greatest emphasis on hygiene and public health; in other words, on prevention of disease rather than its treatment. Throughout his works we find him stressing the importance of (1) dietetics, (2) proper balance between rest and physical exercise, (3) the value of fresh air, sunshine, and salubrious climate, and (4) the inescapable and inseparable connection between morality and physical well-being.

In the third place, Maimonides, contrary to the custom of his times and the traditions of Hippocrates, Galen and other worthies, champions simplicity in pharmacotherapy and recommends administration of simple prescriptions, as against polypharmacy or shotgun prescriptions, extensively employed not only by the ancients but also by many physicians even now. He repeatedly reiterates the paramount value of *Vis Medicatrix Naturae,* to such an extent indeed, that some historians have falsely accused him of therapeutic nihilism. In this connection, I again quote a few lines from one of his works. "Now, most physicians are greatly in error in that they think that medication strengthens the health; it weakens and perverts it; and for this reason hath Aristotle said that most of the patients who die, do so through the medicines of physicians. When the interference of the physician is indicated, his task should be (merely) to sustain the strength of the patient and to promote nature in its effort at repair. Most physicians, however, err in their treatment. In endeavoring to assist nature, they weaken the body with their prescriptions." The far-reaching significance of Rambam's views on etiology, pathology, and therapeutics cannot be exaggerated. Perhaps we may appreciate them more if we recall that, as late as 1796, Dr. S. C. Hahnemann announced his doctrine of Homeopathics. This wizard promulgated the doctrine that all chronic diseases are derived directly or remotely from the itch and contended that it is possible to increase the potency of drugs by attenuating or diluting them all the way to the so-called thirtieth

dilution or potency, which would be one drop of tincture in alcohol or water, sufficient "to envelop the terrestial globe, the
planetary system, and all the stars of first and second magnitude."
Need I add that even now such cults as osteopathy and chiropractic
and so-called "Christian" Science and patent fakirs thrive in our
midst and demand the most drastic legislation for protection of
the public.

In the fourth place, one of the outstanding contributions of Maimonides to the history of medicine is his firm conviction and
emphatic teaching regarding *mens sana in corpore sano,* or the
cultivation of "a healthy mind in a healthy body." Rambam was
one of the earliest physicians to recognize the importance of mental
hygiene, and his work on psychotherapy is a classic in the history
of medicine. This treatise constitutes one of the divisions of his *De
Regimine Sanitatis,* or Makrobiotik, and is spoken of as "Hygiene
of the Soul." It was written for Saladin's son, who suffered from
fits of melancholia. It gives psychotherapeutic advice and rules and
what is especially remarkable, stresses the importance of dietetics
in nervous and psychiatric affections and presents a complete
dietary regimen for such cases. Maimonides regarded the body and
mind as inseparable and mental hygiene just as important as that
of the body. This view extended even to his exegesis of Biblical
passages. Thus, for instance, in commenting upon "He that guar-
deth his mouth and tongue, keepeth his soul from distress" (Proverbs XXI, 23), he interprets the aphorism in both the physical
and the spiritual sense: "He who taketh care of his food and drink,
as well as of his speech (tongue), preserveth both his body and
mind from distress." (The Hebrew word *nefesh* denotes both the
bios, or physical, and the mental life.)

Maimonides' general attitude as a scientist may be best portrayed
perhaps by a translation of one of his epistles to the Jews of
Marseilles.

"Know, my lords, that man ought to believe only one of three
things—first, something which he can clearly grasp through pure
reason as, for instance, the science of arithmetic or geometry or
astronomy; second, something which he can perceive with one
of his five senses as, for instance, when he sees or tastes or hears

or smells or touches; and, third, something which he learns from the prophets and sages of blessed memory, that is, from trustworthy authorities.

"And every man, with common sense, ought to sift and classify, think about and reason over those things which he regards as true and those which he does not, and he should say unto himself, I believe this to be true because I perceive it through my senses, or I believe this to be true through pure reason; or I believe this to be true because I have been told so by the prophets and sages. He, however, who believes a thing which does not fall under any of these three categories, or him it is said, 'The simple believeth everything' (Prov. XIV, 15).

"You should also bear in mind that there are fools who have compiled thousands of books, and that many 'great men'—great in years but not in wisdom—have spent their days in the study of such, and these conceited creatures imagine that those books contain deep wisdom; and so their hearts become elated, and they imagine that they are great and wise because they have learned that wisdom, and it is just in this wherein most, if not all, the world is in error, with the execption of the few."

Unlike the natural scientists of the Victorian age who have smugly and complacently championed the mechanistic or deterministic view of universe and life to the exclusion of all that may be spiritual, Maimonides maintains that, while the scientist should always be guided by his perceptions and logical deductions and inductions, yet there are other things which may not be dreamed of in our philosophies. As Mr. Balfour said, "Science depends on measurement, and things not measurable by yardstick, chemical balance, or other instruments of precision tend to be excluded from its attention. But life and beauty and happiness are not measurable; emotion and intuition and instinct are immensely older than Science and in a comprehensive survey of existence cannot be ignored. Scientists may rightly not consider them in order to do their experimental work but philosophers and physicians cannot."

R. L. Duffus, a modern critic and reviewer, has recently expressed the following thought, "The most civilized minds of our generation are those of scientists who have had the energy and the curiosity to master the humanities." Moses Maimonides undoubtedly belongs to the heroes of this class. His attitude as scientist and physician recalls a similar outlook on life held by another and much later scientist—that great genius of physics, and withal a real man—Michael Faraday, who found time to dedicate to both his oratory and laboratory, although he carefully kept the two apart. He was one of the first to champion and inculcate the doctrine that science and religion are not competitive but, on the contrary, complementary and supplementary; and it is only now, over seven hundred years since Maimonides' time, that scientists of the foremost rank—Jeans, Eddington, Lodge, Millikan, Osborne, Jennings, Einstein, and others—are coming to the same conclusion, that science and Torah must go hand in hand, study of nature and the humanities must advance together, or the whole structure of modern civilization is doomed and will crack up. Well may we in the spirit of Rambam take to heart the doctrine of Koheleth (Eccl. VII. 12), *W'yithron da'ath—ha'hakhmah t'hayeh baaleha,* which may be literally rendered thus:

"The superior excellency of science is—wisdom:
'Tis science taken wisely, science wisely pursued, wisely applied,
That giveth life and maketh life the more worth while."

Those of us who have studied at the Johns Hopkins University will appreciate a striking parallel, which suggests itself to me, between the personality and attainments of Maimonides as physician and scientist and those of one who has contributed most to the fame of the Johns Hopkins Medical School and Hospital—William Osler. Here are two men, standing eight hundred years apart, whose views on science, medicine, and the humanities, whose attitudes toward the deeper problems of life and happiness of fellowmen had much in common. Both Maimonides and Osler combined a thirst for knowledge and love of science with a devotion to the practice of the healing art. Both Osler and Maimonides vehemently stressed the importance of etiology and pathology in studying disease. Both Osler and Rambam advocated simple rational medication to such an extent that they were sometimes styled pharmacologic nihilists, when in reality they were well acquainted with all there was to the materia medica of their times and, realizing acutely the lack of knowledge prevailing on the subject, chose only those simple medicaments the action of which was well established. Both Maimonides and Osler placed most of their reliance on the *Vis Medicatrix Naturae,* or Mother Nature, and believed that prophylaxis and hygiene were even more important than therapeutics. Both emphasized the importance of rest, exercise, fresh air, sunshine, and diet. Both preached and practiced sane morality and sex hygiene as foundations of healthy mind and body. Both Osler and Maimonides, far ahead of the majority of their contemporaries, saw the value of harmonizing science with the humanities. Well may we confer upon Rambam the title of Sir William Osler of mediaeval Arabic and Hebrew medicine. In paying this tribute to his memory, it is only fair to state that he antedated Osler by some seven hundred years. In this connection, a citation from the Talmud (Sanhedrin 108a) may be apropos. In discussing the verse, "These are the generations of Noah; Noah was a righteous and perfect man in his generation; Noah walked with God" (Gen. VI, 1), the question was raised, What is meant by "in his generation?" Rabbi Yohanan answered that Noah was righteous when compared with the standards of his generation but not in comparison with those of later generations. Rabbi Resh Lakish, however, countered with, "If he was perfect in his degenerate times, how much greater would he have been in later generations!"

I deem it most fitting to conclude with the well known so-called prayer of Maimonides. I know full well that recently some have asserted that Rambam did not write this prayer. Who was the author of the prayer is quite irrelevant; the sentiments and lofty ideals it expresses have always been regarded as those of Maimonides. In these our days, when there are groups of creatures belonging to the genus homo (I dare not use the qualifying term *sapiens*) who, blinded by hatred, prejudice, and superstition, reject the achievements of such physicians as Jenner, Koch, Virchow, Ehrlich, Neisser, Wasserman, and von Behring because of their connection (real or fancied) with that great race which gave us the Rambam—I read a metrical translation which I composed thirty years ago, with heightened fervor:

"And now I turn unto my calling;
Oh, stand by me, my God, in this truly important task!
Grant me success! For—
Without Thy loving counsel and support,
Man can avail but naught.
Inspire me with true love for this my art
And for Thy creatures.
Oh, grant—
That neither greed for gain, nor thirst for fame, nor vain
     ambition,
May interfere with my activity.
For these, I know, are enemies of truth and love of men,
And might beguile one in profession
From furthering the welfare of Thy creatures.
Oh, strengthen me!
Grant energy unto both body and the soul,
That I may e'er unhindered, ready be
To mitigate the woes,
Sustain and help,
The rich and poor, the good and bad, the enemy and friend.
Oh, let me e'er behold in the afflicted and the suffering
Only the human being!"

PROBLEMS AND DIFFICULTIES OF UNITED STATES
PSYCHOLOGICAL WARFARE

BY DR. SAUL K. PADOVER

Problems and Difficulties of United States Psychological Warfare

BY DR. SAUL K. PADOVER

PERHAPS the most far-reaching aspect of the current cold war is its concern with world opinion. Each of the major belligerents involved in the unprecedented struggle is making systematic appeals to a global audience that is not yet fully committed to either side. To win the conflict ultimately, each side knows that it must, somehow, influence the minds, emotions, and expectations of an invisible audience that may run as high as two billion people. This is something new in the annals of mankind.

How does the United States fare in this struggle for the minds of men? The answer, as will appear presently, is not encouraging.

Like the Soviet Union, the United States has a large propaganda organization that attempts to influence people abroad. It employs several thousand individuals and uses all the known media for reaching mass audiences. It shows films, maintains libraries, displays posters, distributes pamphlets, and publishes foreign-language magazines. Its radio division, known as the Voice of America, is a world-wide operation with short and medium wave stations in England, Germany, the Philippines, Hawaii, Tangier, and Turkey. The Voice, which has relay stations in many lands, speaks in nearly all foreign languages, including Lithuanian and Georgian.

The voice of America claims a world audience of about 300 million listeners. This is an estimate based on hope. In Western Europe, for example, where the air waves are free, there is a known preference for the much more influential and prestigious BBC. In Soviet-dominated Eastern Europe, the Voice is said to be gaining in influence, but it is hard to tell how much. The Soviet Union itself is all but impenetrable to foreign broadcasts. Since

April, 1949, the Russians have made persistent and seemingly successful efforts to jam broadcasts from abroad. As for Asia, notably China and India, there are so few radio receivers in comparison to the total population that broadcasting efforts, strictly limited in their reach to a few cities, are almost not worth the effort.

In general American propaganda has not made much of a dent in the world's crucial areas. Five major reasons account for the comparative ineffectiveness of American political propaganda abroad.

Egocentrism. Historically, Americans have been so prosperous and such spoiled children of fortune that they have tended to become uncritical about themselves and the world they live in. Implicitly or explicitly, they assume that America has the final answer to everything, that it has solved humanity's age-old problems, and that it is possessor of The Truth in human affairs. American propaganda is, therefore, ethnocentric and fails to understand the mental makeup of the foreign peoples to whom it tries to appeal. Broadcasting Christian Christmas messages to Turkey is a case in point. Hence much of the American output for foreign consumption reads and sounds as if it were designed for Americans. American propaganda tends to talk to itself.

As a rule, Americans do not seem to appreciate the fact that hundreds of millions of people abroad do not think like Americans, live like Americans, or even want to be like Americans. This is particularly true of countries like China, whose basic culture is totally alien to that of America; and of Russia, whose values and institutions are fundamentally different from those of the United States.

Many ancient civilizations, moreover, have a deep respect for their own culture patterns and do not admire those of the United States, which they usually know through Hollywood. The mental image of America, as interpreted through Hollywood films, is certainly not a flattering one. This is particularly true of Grade B and Wild West movies with their fantastic cult of violence. In those films, it will be recalled, every situation—from love to business—is solved through violence, either by fist or by gun.

This certainly gives a strange impression of American mores and democratic values. In addition, the difference in the standard of living between Americans and the overwhelming majority of the world's people, especially non-whites, is so vast as to be unbelievable.

India is a case in point. That vast subcontinent with its 360,000,000 people may well hold the key to the balance of power in Asia, and thereby affect the future security of the United States. For Americans it is a matter of the utmost national concern not to lose India to Communist imperialism. And yet very few Americans understand India, or the rest of Asia, for that matter; and our policy, especially our information policy, in that part of the world is based upon almost fatally wrong suppositions. When we make information or propaganda appeals to the poverty-stricken Indians we talk to them blithely as if they were comfortable, middle-class Americans.

I. *Leadership.* There is no denying that Washington has not offered either the American people or their friends in the world a full measure of leadership. The administration has been either unwilling or unable to clarify and explain its policies, let alone put them in words that stir the conscience and the imagination. Repeatedly our government has made it clear that it is *against* Communism, *against* Sovietism, *against* Stalinism. But, people abroad ask, what is America *for*? Where, they want to know, is America leading us? What kind of world is Washington proposing? Here American propaganda has been all but silent.

II. *Democracy.* Insofar as American propaganda has a central idea, it is democracy. This is implicit in much that is said and written for foreign audiences. There is no question but that democracy—notably the idea of freedom from oppression and from police terror—is potentially an explosive force throughout the world. It is still the greatest enemy of the Communists. But unfortunately the present generation of Americans has not known how "to sell" it to many foreigners. For one thing, the whole concept of democracy is dynamic and flexible; it is not something tailored, "made in America" for export. On the contrary, the democratic ideal, the goal, must be adjusted to national circumstances and to the expectations of foreign audiences. For another, although there is endless talk about democracy, it is nevertheless true that too few Americans really believe in it with the kind of passion and dedication that are needed to carry conviction or to make converts. In this country the democratic triumph has been so complete that the great majority of our people simply take the values and privileges of democracy for granted, as a sort of gift of nature.

What is needed nowadays is a new dedication to the democratic-libertarian ideal in theory and practice, as formulated by Jefferson and Lincoln. Such a spiritual renaissance might do more for our cause abroad than millions of platitudinous words poured out by microphone and mimeograph machines. On a practical level, democracy needs working missionaries, consisting of men and women who would go out among the underprivileged people abroad and serve them in every capacity.

Incidentally, this is what the Communists have done, and are doing, in Asia with skill and success. Their propaganda may be full of lies and their promises cynical, but they do know how to talk to the poor and the miserable, and how to appeal to the aspirations of peoples now struggling for an honorable position among the nations. If we are not to lose a large part of the world by default, we must learn to do likewise.

III. *Ideas*. For some of the reasons that have already been mentioned, the whole propaganda operation of our government suffers from a poverty of ideas. It is, indeed, one of the ironies of our time that in the present ideological world conflict, involving what is in reality a life-and-death struggle between opposing ways of life, the Americans, though they are often on the side of the angels, show themselves to be spiritually so sterile. A really bold and imaginative psychological warfare campaign could find in American civilization, as well as in that of the democratic allies abroad, an inexhaustible and inspiring intellectual arsenal.

In this respect, it should be admitted in all fairness, Americans are the victims of their own inherent decency. The American national character is, by and large, one of directness and straightforwardness. As a rule, Americans lack deviousness; they are basically an honest people. The intellectual subtleties and verbal perversions that are sometimes necessary in propaganda are alien, and sometimes repulsive, to the American mind. This helps to explain why the best contribution that our government has made to the current world-wide propaganda war was what former President Truman called the "campaign of truth." This campaign is based on the uncomplicated and, if I may be permitted to say so, unphilosophical assumption that truth is a simple article that can be easily identified, defined, labeled, and sent around like any package of merchandise. The Truman "campaign of truth" was based upon the charming assumption that all you need to do to counter Communist propaganda is to tell the truth about ourselves. And yet a moment's reflection would show that truth is not a simple proposition; that what is my truth is not your truth; that what appears to be the truth to, say, a Wall Street banker is not the truth to a Chinese coolie; that, in brief, so-called truth often depends upon the angle of vision.

IV. *Racism and imperialism*. Another difficulty in our propaganda effort is connected with American race practices and the white man's imperialism. Though modified by the Supreme Court decision against school segregation, American treatment of the Negro, and other minorities, is well known throughout the world, especially the non-white world. Indeed, people abroad tend to exaggerate the extent of the mistreatment of Negroes and the prejudice against minorities that prevails in the United States. Few foreigners realize that American Negroes have been making solid gains on all fronts—economic, legal, social—in recent years. Abroad only the black racist record is known; the good side is ignored. Here Communist propaganda has, of course, a field day; and unfortunately, it must be admitted that even a little racist evil and prejudice goes a long way abroad. Any act of racism and bias in the United States is always blown up out of all proportion by hostile propaganda and does our country incalculable harm.

For it is clear that mere propagandistic words—sweet-sounding clichés and smooth phrases—are meaningless in the face of reality. When Americans preach democracy and human dignity to, say, Chinese or Indians, the words are apt to have a bitter and even hypocritical sound. For it is no secret from the colored peoples of the world—and there are nearly two billion of them—that even America's Christian churches are hardly "Christian" where non-whites are concerned. It is a shocking truth that less than 1% of America's Christian congregations have mixed membership. The rest practice racial segregation. "The churches," Dr. Liston Pope, head of the Yale University Divinity School, said recently, "have a lot of house cleaning to do before they can call themselves Christians." Dr. Pope told the National Council of the Churches of Christ in the U. S. A. that "Russia's proclamation of racial equality can be combated only by a better demonstration of racial equality than the Soviet can produce." He warned that "if Asia and Africa are totally alienated from the Western nations we shall have lost a major part of our struggle with Russia."[2]

Equally serious, insofar as the effectiveness of our propaganda is concerned, is the feeling that prevails among Asians and Africans that America has taken over the "white man's burden" in regard to imperialism. An increasingly large number of non-white people are convinced that the United States has become the Big Brother of the detested imperialist powers—notably Britain and France—and that American money and military power are now buttressing those decaying and passionately hated empires. Hence some of the dislike that Asians, Africans, and Arabs have for the British and French is beginning to spill over on the Americans. Many non-whites abroad, especially in Asia and the Near East, think that in reality Americans are shrewd hypocrites—that the clever Yankees preach democracy but they really are after oil and other earthly goods.

American policy is thus impaled on the horns of a painful dilemma. The United States is committed to support and maintain France and Britain, but in doing so it alienates the restive colonial peoples. On the other hand, to back openly the legitimate aspirations of the colonial peoples, would be to undermine further the already weakened Western allies and create a power vacuum from which only the Communist could benefit. America is thus in a position of being damned if it does and damned if it doesn't. Here

---

2 *New York Times*, December 13, 1951

is one of the great challenges of our time to our ingenuity, sincerity, and statesmanship. But hitherto, it must be repeated, neither our information policy nor our foreign policy which it reflects has been a sensational success in Asia.

V. *Personnel*. American propaganda has not recruited the most skilled and experienced personnel available in the United States. Quite the contrary seems to be the case. There appears to be a premium on mediocrity, despite the fact that political propaganda, to be successful, requires special sensitivity and unusual skill.

One reason for the non-employment of many of the ablest and most experienced political warfarers is that they are not welcome in Washington. Another reason is more serious, for it runs deeper and affects more people. It has to do with the general political atmosphere. The truth is that under the prevailing conditions of suspicion, and all the phenomena of a nation in a state of confusion and self-doubt, individuals best equipped for psychological warfare work are likely to be the first victims. They are, as a general rule, either too liberal or too sensitive. In the former case, they have difficulty in being accepted or cleared; in the second case, they could not operate freely or well in a political environment that puts a premium on conformism and timidity. Good political propaganda is not a job for the scared or the cautious. It requires men with imagination, with social vision, with bold views.

But, unfortunately, the prevailing atmosphere in the United States today is not always conducive to a free and frank discussion of crucial problems. There is a growing intolerance of unorthodox ideas which—if unchecked—may cost us some of our freedom and security. This is one of the urgent challenges of our time, and we must face it with the utmost courage.

These are, in sum, some of the problems and difficulties which our policy faces. A few of the difficulties may be, at the moment, insoluble. Others can be overcome or improved. In the last analysis nothing is really hopeless. What is required is courage, vision, effort and good will. Given these attributes the most towering obstacles can be surmounted.

In terms of propaganda, the global picture still offers possibilities. As of now, we must keep in mind that a large portion of mankind has not yet taken sides. The one hundred-odd million black Africans have hitherto not cast their lot with East or West, although it is clear that if Boer brutishness is not eradicated in South Africa, the natives there must inevitably hate the West. Similarly the three hundred-odd million Moslems, who are now economically depressed and resentfully anti-West. Nevertheless, the Moslems have not as yet turned to Moscow. Nor have the 360 million Indians, whose general attitude, clearly reflected by Nehru, may be described as a plague o' both your houses. The same is true of hundreds of millions of other peoples in Asia and South America.

Western Europe is more complicated. There anti-American opinion is widespread, although much of it is probably only verbal. Still one cannot ignore the fact that in strategic countries like Italy and France abouth one-third of the electorate votes Communist. Moreover, even among non-Communist West Europeans there exists a good deal of distrust, if not active dislike, of American motives and policies.

This not inconsiderable antipathy for America on the part of so many West Europeans sharply underlines the failure of our policies and propaganda. For it is in Europe, which is closest to us in culture, institutions, and aspirations, that we should have had least difficulty in winning friends and a favorable public opinion. But such has not been the case. In Europe we have not been able to counter the Communist propaganda apparatus, one of the most tireless (and successful) opinion-shaping instruments in the world today. In the face of the vigorous Communist ideological campaign against America, our propaganda has been marked by defensiveness and a lack of clear-cut goals.

It is, indeed, one of the ironies of our time that our propaganda has abandoned the talk about peace to the Communists. The Reds have been permitted to make a virtual monopoly of the world "peace." By a strange twist of fate, it is they who talk peace, and it is we who talk war. Europeans are scared that a jittery America might plunge into World War III which would lead to an atomization of Europe.

The situation can be improved, if some proper steps are taken.

First an independent psychological warfare body should not be subject to the ordinary bureaucratic tests and regulations. It should be given great leeway for action and experimentation, as well as for the choice of personnel.

Second, much of the work that is now done by the thousands of employees in the Office of International Information could be eliminated. There might be, instead, a small body of expert planners who would farm out the necessary work abroad, where, when, and if, necessary. For it has been found that the most persuasive pro-American propaganda is that carried out by foreign friends, directly or indirectly. The most effective American radio operation today, for example, is not the Voice of America but Berlin's station RIAS—Radio in American Sector—which is almost entirely manned and executed by Germans who know how to speak to other Germans. The same may also be said of *Der Monat,* an American-supported German monthly, to which contribute Germany's and Europe's foremost writers and which, consequently, has wide influence among German and other West European intellectuals.

These are, in brief, a few instances of pro-American and anti-Communist operations which can be and should be systematically multiplied. There are pro-American, pro-democratic friends abroad able and willing to wage the ideological battle, if given assistance and encouragement by Washington. Here is an opportunity which the United States ought not to lose.

THE AMERICAN YIDDISH PRESS, A POTENT CIVIC FORCE

BY DR. MORDECAI SOLTES

The American Yiddish Press, A Potent Civic Force

BY DR. MORDECAI SOLTES

THREE YEARS AGO the Yiddish press furnished the first striking example in the centuries of existence of American journalism, of a daily newspaper suspending operation for economic reasons and resuming publication four and a half months later. This was the case with the Jewish Morning Journal, which was founded by the late Jacob Saphirstein over fifty years ago and reached its highest circulation in 1916. Because of financial difficulties the Morning Journal—Daily News shut down on April 10, 1951, but reappeared on the newsstands on August 31, 1951, corroborating my earlier assertion that the readers tend to cling more tenaciously to their Yiddish newspapers than do those of any other foreign language press.

It was published throughout 1952, but was compelled early in 1953 to merge with the Day because of the unusually high cost of production, and is now called the Day-Jewish Journal. It is interesting to note that while the Yiddish press lost one paper between 1923 and 1952 through consolidation, the 18 daily English newspapers in New York City lost twelve during the same period. The general newspapers which were absorbed or ceased publication altogether, are: New York American, Call, Globe, Herald, Mail, P.M., Press, Star, Morning and Evening Sun, Morning and Evening World.

The ushering in of 1951, midpoint in the 20th century, also marked significant milestones in American Yiddish journalism— the 8oth anniversary of the founding of the first two Yiddish periodicals—the *Yiddishe Zeitung* and the *Post* by I. K. Buchner and Zevi Hirsh Bernstein (1870) , and the 65th anniversary of the establishment of the first Yiddish daily, the *Tageblatt* (1885) , by Kasriel H. Sarasohn, which was absorbed in 1928 by the Morning Journal. Notwithstanding the fact that Yiddish was the prevailing tongue used by millions of our East European brethren, it was not until 1903 that the first Yiddish daily, *Der Freind,* was founded in St. Petersburg. To have anticipated European Jewry in the genesis of the Yiddish daily press by eighteen years, is a reflection of the dynamic spirit of enterprise and resourcefulness which are part and parcel of the American character.

The pioneering efforts in Yiddish journalism did not prove rewarding in the initial period. The American soil was not prepared for this type of venture. The fact that very few of the Jewish immigrants had read newspapers in their native lands, made the task of the leaders of the Yiddish newspapers exceedingly difficult. For they had to cultivate the habit of purchasing and reading papers among the newcomers, and thus create their own reading public. The major factor in attracting new readers was the simplification and popularization of the Yiddish language which had been held in low esteem by the intellectual Jews in old Russia, who looked upon it as a mere jargon intended exclusively for those who were ignorant of the Hebrew language. This erroneous attitude was transplanted to America and retarded the growth of the press in its early stages. For the Judeo-German employed by the writers of those days was cumbersome. In due course there was a transformation in outlook. Yiddish was utilized effectively by the leaders of both the labor and Zionist movements, as well as in literary circles, to reach a larger number of followers. Thereafter the number of readers increased rapidly, the circulation of the daily press growing from 3,750 in 1885 to 537,982 in 1916, when it reached the highest level of its numerical strength and influence.

Thus the Yiddish language press and literary creativity were destined to reach the acme of their growth and expansion upon the North American continent. From the beginning Yiddish had been borrowing words from the languages of the people among whom the Jews dwelt. It therefore bears the imprint of every country in which Jews found homes the past few hundred years. This tendency is common to all living tongues. It is by this process, for example, that English has become "richer and deeper". As the late Louis Marshall, native-born American Jewish leader, aptly put it: "The outstanding property of a language is that it borrows and takes—unscrupulously. It does not waste thought on whether this belongs to it or it doesn't . . . While Hebrew, for example, was not used, it remained pure and untouched and isolated. When it became a vital medium of speech, is began to absorb and assimilate from many sources, hundreds and hundreds of new words . . . Ever since my youth I have read Yiddish. I learned it was essential in my work. There are few people who realize what a great and brilliant literature has been written in Yiddish. It is immense."

Having reared their own generation of readers who turned to the Yiddish newspapers constantly for information and guidance in the solution of varied problems of a civic, vocational, social, and personal character, it was inevitable that there should have grown up close and lasting bonds of association between the two. As a result, the readers have been known to support their group press more generously and for a longer period than have the non-Jewish immigrants. This has been true particularly of the Jewish workers. While the American labor movement has not been able to maintain any daily newspaper of its own, Jewish laborers have developed the largest and most powerful foreign language newspaper, the Jewish Daily Forward, which has utilized its surplus to establish a labor radio station, WEVD, and to subsidize English labor dailies.

From time to time, particularly when our country is at war, questions are raised regarding the function and desirability of the immigrant press in America. Some extremists have even gone so far as to propose that it be abolished altogether, or, at least, as a Senator and Congressman from Georgia proposed, that the foreign language newspapers be required to print in an adjoining parallel column an exact English translation of the text, a regulation which would have been tantamount to putting them out of business.

What are the implications of such extreme proposals? They are clear. Apparently the conclusion is inevitable that foreign language newspapers are disloyal and inimical to the welfare of our country. They must therefore be carefully watched and checked, censored, or eliminated altogether. Do the facts support such extreme views? Well, my doctorate dissertation at Teachers College, Columbia University, was undertaken in an effort to lift this question out of the realm of conjecture, prejudice and speculation to that of objective research, analysis and evaluation. I regarded it as timely to undertake about three decades ago a survey of the Yiddish press, a most important segment of the foreign language press, from the point of view of the civic influence which is exerted.

When I made this inquiry, there were 1500 foreign language newspapers and magazines in the United States, with a total circulation of about eight million. What a potential power for good or evil in moulding public opinion this press represented. Professor Snedden, chairman of my thesis committee, urged me "to put it on a statistical basis, so that sociologists throughout the country may respect your findings and not tend to dismiss them as the personal views and opinions of the writer." Following Prof. Snedden's advice, I proceeded to assemble information regarding the contents of over 1500 editorials which had appeared in the Yiddish dailies during a period of six months. To avoid having the significant events of any particular period overshadow the content of the editorials, and to obtain a normal, representative sampling, the six months were chosen at random from different years. I also excluded the period during which the United States was an active participant in the World War and the censorship was operative.

Specifically, I was interested in determining what types of problems the editorials treated, and what attitudes individual newspapers and the press as a whole assumed towards the more important issues raised; in other words, to establish the volume and nature of the civic influence radiated by the Yiddish press by means of its editorial columns. The statistical survey established conclusively that the editorials were devoted primarily to a consideration of American issues. An examination of the list of items which constituted subjects of editorial comment and the frequency of treatment of each particular theme, led inevitably to the conclusion that the Yiddish press was keenly responsive to the outstanding needs and problems facing American Jewry; that the questions most frequently treated were those which had moved American Jewry to action. Moreover, a detailed analysis of the distribution of the entire volume of the editorial content showed that about 64% were devoted to general American issues, 26% to problems of a specifically Jewish nature, and 10% to foreign or world questions.

Throughout the 68 years of their existence the Yiddish dailies have rendered a highly important service in interpreting and adjusting their immigrant readers to the complex American environment, and vice versa. They have also served as a potent influence in elevating the cultural taste and level of their reading clientele. One of the distinguishing characteristics of the Yiddish press is its practice of devoting an unusually large proportion of its space to solid reading material such as does not normally find its way into the average daily newspaper, but which goes rather into the American magazine or literary journal. In fact, a scientific study of the contents of 17 daily papers in New York (5 in English, 3 in German, 5 in Italian and 4 in Yiddish) conducted by Columbia University students in sociology under Prof. Tenney, established that the Yiddish newspapers are not only conveyors of news but rank the highest in the amount of space devoted to cultural items (52%) *. The columns of these newspapers have afforded outlets to talented Yiddish writers the world over. Some of the gifted authors had already established reputations for themselves in the literary centers of their countries of origin, while others gained prominence through this fruitful instrumentality. Thus, the Yiddish press enriched American Jewish life and helped create a new cultural center, a new reservoir of spiritual influence in this land.

In the past few years the Yiddish newspapers have again demonstrated their eagerness to welcome the recent arrivals who escaped the horrible fate of Nazi savagery. They set aside special pages and introduced new features of direct concern to the post-war immigrants, in the hope of facilitating their incorporation

* Shriver, W.P.—"Immigrant Forces"—p.227

into the living stream of American life. Thus, the Yiddish papers have consciously striven to implant in their hearts sentiments of esteem and appreciation of their new country, to familiarize them with its variegated life and resources and the guiding democratic principles in which our government is firmly rooted.

An interesting sidelight is the question regarding the extent to which the editorial articles are read by the various occupational groups. Some light was shed by an inquiry involving two sets of readers which revealed the astounding result that Jewish laborers follow the editorial comment most regularly, with professionals and merchants tied for second place and housewives the least interested. It is my considered judgment that a similar inquiry, if conducted at the present time, would disclose that, while women still prefer fiction, they have extended their reading interests in substantial numbers to more serious discussions, and that a greater proportion of all the readers invariably turn to the editorials and columnists for guidance in the formulation of their views on vital issues.

A section of my study was devoted to a resume of the prevailing attitudes of the Yiddish press towards half a dozen major civic questions, with quotations from editorials. One of them, that of Urban Congestion, received a great deal of community attention in the first two decades of this century. Commenting on the favorable attitude which the Yiddish press assumed towards the efforts made by agencies to stimulate Jewish settlement on farms, I posed this question, "Why has the immigrant Jew hesitated to leave the congested areas to become a farmer?" To which I replied as follows: "Aside from the historic reason that the Jew has been constantly driven off the soil and has been prevented for centuries from owning and cultivating land, additional deterring factors are discussed frankly in the editorial columns of the Yiddish press. One of the causes of the reluctance of Jewish parents to settle upon the farm has been the lack of adequate educational facilities —both general and Jewish—for the young children, in the sparsely populated agricultural sections, as well as the limited opportunities for social intercourse for the young men and women. This lack of spiritual anchorage has prevented those Jews who are anxious to continue Jewish life and who are deeply concerned about the education of their children, from carrying into effect their desire to settle upon the land. Despite these discouraging conditions and circumstances, however, the Yiddish press continually urges the Jew to become a tiller of the soil, emphasizing the fact that the difficulties can be overcome by persistent, united efforts."

It is interesting to note that Dr. Gabriel Davidson in his book, "Our Jewish Farmers," in appraising frankly the normal and unique difficulties confronting Jews who are anxious to renew their direct contacts with the soil, points to the same major deterring factor. Religious and social Centers have sprung up, however, in recent years in farming communities of substantial Jewish population, particularly in the East and Middle West, indicating convincingly that this challenging obstacle is not insurmountable. Of course this progressive point of view of the Yiddish papers has not altered. They are quick to detect and encourage the desire of Jews to return to the land. They direct attention to the factors which are contributing towards the creation of a healthy Jewish farming population, and speak with pride of the fact that the Jewish trend has been towards the soil, notwithstanding the opposite tendency away from the soil apparent in this country in recent decades.

My prediction in 1923 concerning the probable future of the Yiddish press, grew out of an incidental by-product of the investigation of the types of readers whom it reached. It was found that a high proportion of the latter who are at home with the English language continued, nevertheless, to read Yiddish dailies. The following question: "If you can read newspapers printed in English, state for what special reasons you read Yiddish newspapers," elicited replies that were revealing. About 20% advanced sentimental reasons, such as their attachment to their "mother tongue" and their eagerness for its preservation. Over 80% who read English just as fluently or with greater facility, indicated that they turned to the Yiddish dailies primarily for Jewish news and discussions of specific Jewish problems, which, they claimed, were not treated adequately in the general press.

On the basis of the above replies, I expressed the following view: "Although the Jewish immigrants support their group press more generously and for a longer period than do the non-Jewish immigrants, the present tendencies, if maintained, point to the gradual decline of the Yiddish press in this country." At the final oral examination, Professor Kandel asked me whether the same applies to the future of Yiddish literature in the United States. In my reply I made a differentiation which still holds, between a daily newspaper which must function in the everyday life of its readers, bringing them the news promptly, helping them to obtain jobs, and literary creativity which does not depend upon such factors for its existence and growth. The inspired poet or author who is prompted to create in Yiddish or Hebrew is not confronted with the immediate question of the next morning's sales, as is the newspaper publisher, whose business involves large investments, the setting up of intricate machinery, and the like.

The late Peter Wiernik, in the last decade of the 19th century, prognosticated the end of the Yiddish press in America within a quarter of a century. Instead, the circulation grew by leaps and bounds, reaching the peak of its development in 1916. I have been more cautious and have made my prediction with greater reserve. There may be blood transfusions in the future which will tend to prolong its span of existence and usefulness. It should be borne in mind that the actual number of persons who read these papers is substantially larger than the total number of copies sold. In the questionnaire which I submitted to the readers of the Yiddish press I inquired regarding the number of additional members of their families or friends who read the daily which they purchase. The results showed that the circulation figures would have to be augmented by about 75%. This figure would have to be further increased to-day when the price of a Yiddish daily has gone up to 7c per copy on weekdays and 15c on Sundays.

I have no hesitancy in asserting that regardless of the length of the period during which the Yiddish press is destined to function among us, the judgment of history will pronounce it a constructive, dynamic force in American Jewish life . . . It has not only helped to fructify and enrich Jewish cultural creativity by opening its columns to talented literary artists and creative souls the world over; but it has also rendered a vital historical service during a critical period of transition from the old to the new environment, by consciously striving to facilitate the incorporation of the newcomers into the living stream of American life, civicly, socially, and economically. Those associated with this influential segment of American journalism may take justifiable pride in the record of valuable service to our country and to our brethren both here and abroad which it has to its credit.

The deep concern of American Jewry regarding the future of Yiddish which was "elevated from a folk language to a nationally recognized vehicle of cultural expression, and is still a creative and dynamic force in many communities of the free world," is reflected in the resolution adopted by the Rabbinical Assembly at its Convention in 1953, urging its members "to do all in their power individually and collectively, to support and encourage the future development of the Yiddish press and publications." Moreover, the Statistical Abstract of the United States for 1952, reports in Table No. 31—"White Population, By Mother Tongue"—that in 1940 there were 1,751,000 or 1.5% of the American population who considered Yiddish as their mother tongue.*

---

* From my article on the Yiddish Press in "The New International 1954 Year Book", p. 613

PSYCHOSOMATIC MEDICINE

BY EDWARD WEISS, M.D.

Psychosomatic Medicine

BY EDWARD WEISS, M.D.

PSYCHOSOMATIC (psyche: spirit and soma: body) is a new term to describe the relationship between the emotions and bodily illness, but it represents an approach to medicine as old as the art of healing itself. Medicine has always recognized that such a relationship existed, but in the last century the advances in laboratory medicine and the emphasis on organic disease have been responsible for a neglect of the emotional life in the study of illness. Moreover, until the advent of the psychoanalytic method originated by Sigmund Freud no satisfactory technique for the study of human behavior existed. Therefore, the subject of psychosomatic medicine—which believes that bodily disorders can be understood only when emotional factors are investigated in addition to physical factors—had to wait upon the development of our knowledge regarding the application of psychoanalysis to medicine. The fusion of the two streams of knowledge, that is, the advances in physical medicine and the contributions of psychological medicine, makes up what is known as psychosomatic medicine. It is not a new specialty but rather an approach which applies to all aspects of medicine and surgery. It may be defined as the simultaneous application of physiologic and psychologic techniques in the study of the patient in an effort to reach a definitive diagnosis for the purpose of comprehensive medical care. In other words, it does not mean less study of the body; it only means more study of the emotional life. As a science, psychosomatic medicine aims at discovering the precise nature of the relationship between the emotions and bodily illness.

Following the discoveries of Freud, Deutsch in Europe and Jelliffe in America applied the principles of psychoanalysis to general medical problems and paved the way for later systematic studies. Draper (1928) anticipated the term psychosomatic by referring to disease as a *psysomatic* reaction. Alexander and his associates of the Chicago Institute of Psychoanalysis, beginning about 1932, made psychosomatic studies of gastrointestinal disorders, hypertension, bronchial asthma, and more recently arthritis. A little later Wolff and his co-workers began their physiologic investigations of the relationship of the emotions and bodily changes in a wide variety of disorders—headache, especially migraine, stomach disorders, and heart disease—and in 1935 Dunbar collected the widely scattered literature in this field in a book devoted to the subject. Halliday contributed many articles from a public health standpoint and was largely responsible for calling attention to the emotional component in rheumatism. His studies of psychosomatic disorders among the insured population of Scotland might be referred to as a socio-dynamic approach to chronic illness. The Journal of Psychosomatic Medicine began publication in 1939 and the American Society for Research in Psychosomatic Problems was established in 1942. Weiss and English published a textbook on Psychosomatic Medicine in 1943 and a fund for research in this subject was sponsored by the National Committee for Mental Hygiene in 1944. A clinic for graduate training in psychoanalysis and psychosomatic medicine was established at Columbia University in 1945.

A great impetus was given to the subject as a result of medical experiences in World War II. The large number of psychoneurotic individuals discovered in the selective service process and the disabilities caused by emotional factors in military training and combat impressed every physician. Indeed, it might well be said that World War I established psychiatry on a firm scientific basis and World War II saw its more complete integration into general medicine. When that integration is complete it is possible that we will have little need for the term psychosomatic because good medicine will be psychosomatic.

The gastro-intestinal (digestive) tract is, above all other systems, the pathway through which emotions are often expressed in behavior. The abdomen aptly has been called the sounding board of the emotions. Why this is so becomes apparent when we consider that the infant's first contact with the world is through the mouth, so that the processes of feeding and feeling must relate themselves to one another. Therefore, upon the love and security, or anxiety and insecurity, which become associated with the nursing process will depend many of the psychosomatic relationships of adult life, called forth by events which awaken old associations.

Based upon these considerations Alexander and his associates laid the foundations (1934) for understanding many of the disturbances of gastrointestinal function in terms of certain trends within the personality. Studying the unconscious mental life of patients with digestive disturbances, whom many clinical observers had referred to as hard driving, tense, and ambitious, they discover just the opposite kind of striving—an unconscious desire for passivity and dependence. They believe that these latter repressed tendencies act as a stimulus to the stomach, leading to a disturbance of function, which produces symptoms of indigestion.

In a study of a modern Alexis St. Martin, who had an opening of the stomach in the abdominal wall as a result of an operation, Wolf and Wolff observed the changes in the stomach concurrent with certain feeling states such as fear and anger. They noted alterations in stomach motility, secretion, and circulation.

French and his associates studied bronchial asthma from a psychological standpoint, correlating attitudes of anger and hostility toward the mother with the fear of being abandoned.

One of the most fundamental relationships in psychosomatic medicine is that which exists between the glands of internal secretion and the personality. Benedek and Rubinstein, studying cellular changes in the vaginal tract at the same time that the behavior of the patient was being minutely observed by means of the psychoanalytic method, noted the close connection between sexual behavior and glandular function.

Growing out of Pavlov's work (1900) on conditioned reflexes and Cannon's observations (1915) regarding the physiological effects of fear, hunger, pain, and rage, the important subject of experimental neuroses in animals promises to throw light on human behavior and illness (Gantt, Liddell, Massermann).

Psychotherapy, which may be major or minor, is an essential part of the psychosomatic concept. The general physician must learn to administer minor psychotherapy, and recognize the indications for major psychotherapy, referring such patients to psychiatrists.

The essential requirements for this development are taking place: 1) adequate preparation in the social sciences, as well as in the physical sciences, for the premedical student; 2) adequate attention to psychopathology as well as to tissue pathology in medical education; and 3) the development of divisions of psychiatry within general hospitals. Until we have physical proximity of psychiatry and medicine we cannot hope for the complete integration which is essential for the psychosomatic concept.

References

1. Alexander, F.: Ten Year Report, Inst. for Ps., Chicago, Ill., 1942.
2. Benedek, T. and Rubenstein, R. B.: The Sexual Cycle in Women, Psm. Med. Monograph, Paul B. Hober, N.Y., 1942.
3. Deutsch, Felix: Die Bedeutung Psychoanalytischer Kenntnisse fur die inner Medizin. Mitt. d. Ges. f. innere Med. U. Kinderheil, in Wien 21, p. 23-24, 1922.
4. Draper, George: Disease, a Psychosomatic Reaction, J.A.M.A., 90, p. 1281-1284, 1928.
5. Dunbar, H. F.: Emotions and Bodily Changes, Columbia Univ. Press, N.Y., 1935.
6. French, T. M. and Alexander, F.: Psychogenic Factors in Bronchial Asthma, Psm. Med. Monograph, Paul B. Hoeber, N.Y., 1941.
7. Halliday, J. L.: The Rising Incidence of Psychosomatic Illness, Lancet, V. 2, 11, July 2, 1938.
8. Jelliffe, Smith Ely: Psychoanalysis and internal medicine. In: Psychoanalysis Today, Ed. S. Lorand, N.Y., Covici-Friede, p. 293-306, 1933.
9. Weiss, E. and English, O. S.: Psychosomatic Medicine, W. B. Saunders Co., 1949, 2nd. edit., Phila.
10. Wolf, S. and Wolff, H. G.: Evidence on the Genesis of Peptic Ulcer in Man, J.A.M.A., 120, 670, Oct. 31, 1942.

ADDRESSES BEFORE JEWISH ACADEMY OF ARTS AND SCIENCES—
1934-1954

Addresses Before
Jewish Academy of Arts and Sciences—
1934-1954

Nov. 25, 1934   Daniel Frohman: "Reminiscences of the Theatre"

Mar. 3, 1935   Prof. Richard Gottheil: "On the Teaching of Semitics"

Apr. 28, 1935   Prof. Jekuthiel Ginsburg: "Maimonides as Astronomer and Mathematician"

Prof. David I. Macht: "Maimonides as Scientist and Physician"

Prof. Chaim Tchernowitz: "Maimonides as Halakist and Scholastic"

June 30, 1935   Dr. A. A. Roback: "Race and Mode of Expression"

Dec. 15, 1935   Judge Irving Lehman: "Problems of Jurisprudence"

Prof. Ludwig Lewisohn: "American Literature of Jewish Interest"

Prof. Franz Oppenheimer: "The European Impasse"

Jan. 26, 1936   Dr. Morris Fishbein: "Exposing Medical Follies"

Mar. 22, 1936   Dr. Albert Einstein: "The Calling of the Jews"

Prof. Israel Davidson: "On Medieval Jewish Studies"

May 24, 1936   Prof. A. W. Binder: "Recent Jewish Contributions to Music"

Prof. Chaim Tchernowitz: "The History of Jewish Law"

Prof. Morris Raphael Cohen: "Jews in Recent Philosophy"

Dec. 6, 1936   Prof. Arthur Nussbaum: "Problems of Law"

Mar. 21, 1937   Dr. David I. Macht: "The Bible as a Source Book for Experimental Research Problems in Science"

May 23, 1937   Dr. A. A. Roback: "Euphemistic Phrases Among the Jews"

Nov. 21, 1937   Prof. Guido Kisch: "German Jews and the World of Science"

Jan. 23, 1938   Dr. A. A. Brill: "The Problem of Determinism as Viewed by the Psychiatrist"

Dr. Abraham Myerson: "Eugenics—A Critical Survey"

Mar. 20, 1938   Dr. Samuel Belkin: "Jewish Law Among the Palestinian and Hellenistic Jews"

May 22, 1938   Prof. Ludwig Lewisohn: "Jewish Literature in the Diaspora"

Rabbi Abraham Burstein: "Judaic Elements in Early American Literature"

Nov. 20, 1938   Prof. Morris R. Cohen, Jacob Shatzky, and Rabbi Samuel Schulman: "Philosophies of Jewish History"

Feb. 6, 1939   Prof. Ismar Elbogen: "What is Jewish Literature"

Dr. Samuel Belkin: "Judaism as a Democratic Theocracy"

Mar. 20, 1939   Dr. Harry Friedenwald: "A Marrano's Views of Jewish Matters with a note on the Jews' Contribution to the Study of Astronomy in the Middle Ages"

May   22, 1939   Prof. Richard Krautheimer: "Ancient Syna-
gogues and their Relation to Roman and
Early Christian Architecture"

Nov.   27, 1939   Dr. Joshua Trachtenberg: "The Demonic Jew:
an Investigation into the Sources of Medi-
eval Anti-Semitism"

Jan.   22, 1940   Prof. Morris R. Cohen: "The Future of Jewish
Studies"

May   27, 1940   Rev. Dr. Leo Jung: "Rashi As Interpreter"

Dec.   1, 1940   Dr. David I. Macht: "Recent Experimental Researches of Biblical Interest" (Illustrated)

Jan.   29, 1941   Prof. Paul Klapper: "Contemporary Education"

Mar.   23, 1941   Dr. A. S. E. Yahuda: "Is the Bible or Critical
View of the Bible Right About the Early
History of Israel?"
Dr. A. A. Roback: "Jewish Personality"
Aaron Copland: "Contemporary Music"

May   28, 1941   Prof. Max M. Laserson: "European Conflicts"

Nov.   10, 1941   Prof. Franz Boas: "The Race Problem"

Jan.   26, 1942   Dr. Julius Burstein: "Why We Get Heart
Disease"
Dr. Elihu Katz: "Why Dyspepsia—Its Nature
and Cause"
Dr. Albert Ashton Berg: "Some Remarks on
Cancer of the Stomach"

Mar.   26, 1942   Frederick Jacobi: "Some Aspects of Contemporary Music"
Prof. Curt Sachs: Report on his forthcoming
book, "The Rise of Music in the Ancient
World—East and West"

May   25, 1942   Prof. Abraham A. Neuman: "The Jews of Medieval Spain"

Mar.   2, 1943   Dr. Salo W. Baron: "The Doctrine of Religious Martyrdom and its Influence on Jewish History"

May   24, 1943   Joseph Yasser: "Renaissance in Jewish Music"

Nov. 22, 1943   Leon Huhner: " A Jewish Pioneer in Early Florida"

Franklin P. Adams: "Early Days"

Mar. 28, 1944   Dr. Nissim Touroff: "Nations as Personalities"

June   6, 1944   Rev. Dr. Leo Jung: "More Mistranslations as Sources of Law and Folklore"

Nov. 29, 1944   Dr. Simon Halkin: "Dominant Socio-Historical Ideas in Modern Hebrew Literature"

Jan. 23, 1945   Dr. Moses Jung: "An Inter-Cultural Project— in New England"

Dr. Mordecai Soltes: "Some Observations on the Development of the Yiddish Press in New York during the Past Quarter Century"

May   28, 1945   Dr. Nissim Touroff: "Reeducating the German People"

Dr. Kalman Friedman: "Italian Jewry, Past, Present and Future"

Nov. 27, 1945   Dr. Morris Meister: "Science-Talented Youth in a Free Society"

Mar. 27, 1946   Dr. Max Weinreich: "The Role of German Scholarship in Nazi Crimes against the Jews"

Nov. 26, 1946   Dr. John D. Gordan: "An Exhibition of Browning Material from the Berg Collection of the New York Public Library"

Dr. Samuel H. Goldenson: "Interpretation of Robert Browning's Thought with Special Reference to Jewish Themes"

Mar. 25, 1947   Dr. Abraham I. Katsh: "The Relationship between the Talmud and the Koran"

May   20, 1947   Dr. Edward Weiss: "Psychosomatic Medicine"

Dr. Hyman Grinstein: "The Jew and Judaism in the American Environment"

Nov.   25, 1947   Dr. Jacob I. Hartstein: "Yeshiva Education in America"

William B. Herlands: "Some Needed Reforms in the Conduct of Congressional and Other Legislative Investigations"

Jan.   27, 1948   Dr. A. A. Roback: "World-Concept in Jewish Folklore"

Dr. George Lawton: "On Being a Good Jew"

Dr. Joshua Finkel: "Abraham, Melchizedek, and the Kings of Sodom (Gen. XIV) : A Study of the Laws and Customs of the Time"

Mar.   29, 1948   Dr. Louis M. Epstein: "Traditional Jewish Standards of Sex Morality"

May   25, 1948   Prof. Chaim Tchernowitz: "The Unity of Philosophy and Halachah in Maimonides"

Nov.   23, 1948   Dr. Hymen Alpern: "Jews in Latin-American Literature"

Jan.   25, 1949   Chaplain Abraham Burstein: "Jews in Prison"

Mar.   23, 1949   Dr. Benjamin Fine: "Discriminatory and Other Aspects of Higher Education in America"

May   24, 1949   Dr. A. A. Roback: "A Jewish Culture Without the Jewish People"

Jan.   24, 1950   Prof. M. M. Laserson, Prof. A. I. Katsh, Rabbi A. Burstein: "The State of Israel"

Mar.   28, 1950   Prof. Hans Kohn: "Teaching in America"

May   16, 1950   Rev. Dr. Leo Jung: "Three Problems Between Man and God"

Prof. Morton Gottschall: "Twenty-five Years as a College Dean"

Nov. 14, 1950   Dr. Yehuda Kohn: "Constitutional Problems in Israel"

Jan. 16, 1951   Prof. Mark Wischnitzer: "Jewish Guilds in Antiquity and the Middle Ages"

Apr.   4, 1951   Prof. Pablo Link: "Jews in South America: History and Prospects"

May   28, 1951   Dr. Bernhard Blumenkranz: "Jewish-Christian Polemics in the First Century"

Nov. 26, 1951   Prof A. A. Roback: "The Quandary of the Jewish Instructor in the Social Sciences"

Jan. 29, 1952   Prof. Saul K. Padover: "Problems and Difficulties of United States Psychological Warfare"

Mar. 25, 1952   Rev. Dr. Robert Gordis: "Ecclesiastes: Most Modern Book in the Bible"

May   20, 1952   Prof. Nelson Glueck: "The Jordan River" (Illustrated)

Nov. 25, 1952   Dr. Joseph Diamond: "Discoveries in Modern Medicine"

Mar. 24, 1953   Dr. David Petegorsky: "The Crisis of the Jewish Community"

May   26, 1953   Prof. Otto Klineberg: "The Scientific Study of National Characteristics"

Nov. 24, 1953   Dr. Henry W. Simon: "Publishing: Business or Profession"

Mar. 23, 1954   Dr. Hirsch Leib Gordon: "Psychiatry in Bible, Talmud and Zohar"

May   25, 1954   Prof. Harry M. Orlinsky: "Jewish Influence on Christian Translations of the Bible"

OFFICERS, MEMBERS, AND FELLOWS OF THE ACADEMY

LEO JUNG, *President*

SAMUEL WEISS ⎱ *Vice-Presidents*
A. A. NEUMAN ⎰

HYMEN ALPERN, *Treasurer*

ABRAHAM BURSTEIN, *Secretary*
46 West 83rd Street
New York 24, N. Y.

BOARD OF GOVERNORS
OFFICERS and:

ALEXANDER BRODY
JACOB I. HARTSTEIN
MOSES JUNG
ABRAHAM I. KATSH

GUIDO KISCH
DAVID I. MACHT
A. A. ROBACK
MORDECAI SOLTES

*Members and Fellows**

Franklin Pierce **Adams***
Hymen **Alpern**
Salo W. **Baron***
Samuel **Belkin***
Adele **Bildersee**
Joshua **Bloch***
Alexander **Brody**
Abraham **Burstein**
Julius **Burstein**
Israel **Chipkin**
Albert **Einstein***
J. D. **Eisenstein***
Benjamin **Fine**
Joshua **Finkel**
Louis **Finkelstein***
Maurice **Finkelstein**
Walter J. **Fischel***
Morris **Fishbein***
Felix **Frankfurter***
Solomon B. **Freehof**
Emanuel **Gamoran**
Nelson **Glueck***
Robert **Gordis**
Hirsch L. **Gordon**

Morton **Gottschall**
Milton **Handler**
Jacob I. **Hartstein**
Abraham J. **Heschel**
Leon **Huhner***
Leo **Jung**
Moses **Jung**
Abraham I. **Katsh**
Elihu **Katz**
Charles E. H. **Kauvar***
Guido **Kisch***
Otto **Klineberg**
Hans **Kohn***
Richard **Krautheimer**
George **Lawton**
Rufus **Learsi**
Jacob **Letschinsky***
Walter **Levy**
Ludwig **Lewisohn***
William **Liebermann***
H. L. **Lurie**
David I. **Macht***
Jacob R. **Marcus**
Morris **Meister**

Members and Fellows* (Continued)

Abraham A. Neuman*

Arthur Nussbaum*

Harry M. Orlinsky

George G. Ornstein

Saul K. Padover

David W. Petegorsky

A. A. Roback*

Morrie Ryskind

Curt Sachs*

Samuel Schulman*

I. L. Sharfman*

Abba Hillel Silver

Henry W. Simon

Mordecai Soltes

Abel G. Warshawsky*

Max Weinreich

Edward Weiss*

Samuel Weiss

Mark Wischnitzer*

Harry A. Wolfson*

Corresponding Members

Argentina: Pablo Link

England: Selig Brodetzky
             S. Marmorstein
             Cecil Roth

Mexico: Salomon Cahan

Israel: Jacob Ettinger
         Simon Halkin
         Isaac Herzog
         J. Kliegler
         Yehuda Kohn
         Lazarus Zwisohn